Donaldson of the 94th—Scots Brigade

Donaldson of the 94th—Scots Brigade

The Recollections of a Soldier During the Peninsula & South of France Campaigns of the Napoleonic Wars

Joseph Donaldson

LEONAUR

Donaldson of the 94th—Scots Brigade: the Recollections of a Soldier During the Peninsula & South of France Campaigns of the Napoleonic Wars
by Joseph Donaldson

Originally published in 1838 under the title
Recollections of the Eventful Life of a Soldier

Published by Leonaur Ltd

Text in this form and material original to this edition
copyright © 2008 Leonaur Ltd

ISBN: 978-1-84677-444-7 (hardcover)
ISBN: 978-1-84677-443-0 (softcover)

http://www.leonaur.com

Publisher's Notes

Contents

Introduction

The ensuing narrative, from its outset to its close in 1814, embraces a period of about twenty-one years, fifteen of which relate to the author's boyhood, and the remaining six to his career in the army. The only part of the soldier's story which begets a feeling of disappointment is its abrupt termination. The vicissitudes of his subsequent career might have formed an interesting, though melancholy, sequel to the present volume. The few particulars we have gathered refer chiefly to that period of his life.

While in Ireland in 1814, about a year previous to the conclusion of the narrative, the author married the individual of whom, under the name of Ellen McCarthy, he speaks in such high terms of admiration. By this union he became the father of ten children, seven of whom died in early life. In 1815, he returned with his family to Glasgow, where he under went various changes of fortune, more particularly adverted to in the narrative, which induced him "to resume the uniform of a soldier." He accordingly embarked with his family for London, and enlisted in the service of the East India Company, in which he was soon promoted to the rank of recruiting sergeant. This occupation, while, contrary to his wishes, it imposed on him the duty of remaining in this country, afforded facilities for indulging those literary and scientific predilections which had distinguished him in the Peninsula; and he now endeavoured to turn them to advantage by the study of anatomy and medicine. Thus occupied, he remained in London, until, in 1817, he was removed to

Glasgow, where he began and completed writing from memory the interesting *Recollections* which form the first portion of this volume, the proceeds of which enabled him still farther to prosecute his studies at the University, where, "exchanging the tartan for the broadcloth," he mingled unobserved among the other students. In consequence of his great dislike to the revolting practices which at that time characterized the recruiting service, he applied to Captain William Marshall, Superintendent of the East India Company in Edinburgh, who, through the influence of Colonel Hastings, got him transferred to the situation of head-clerk in the Glasgow Military District Office, where he remained for some years. In 1827, having procured his discharge, he was enabled, on the trifling proceeds of his literary labours, and by dint of severe economy and close application, to take the degree of surgeon. Shortly afterwards, he removed to the town of Oban, in Argyllshire, where he continued to practise his new profession with as much success as a field so circumscribed would permit, till the year 1829, when, wearied with the proverbial drudgery of such a life, and anxious to give greater scope to his talents, he once more embarked for London, leaving his wife and children in Scotland. With " manners and dispositions not framed in the world's school," it is scarcely matter of surprise that in such a place as the metropolis he failed to procure the employment he sought. He remained there several months, occasionally solacing his dreary hours with that species of literary composition which was his chief delight. Besides contributions to periodicals, he completed a work, entitled *Life in Various Circumstances*, which, had not the MS. been unfortunately lost with other property, on its way from France two years afterwards, might have precluded the necessity of this brief and imperfect notice. Unsuccessful in London, he proceeded to Paris, where, while attending the anatomical academies, he died in October, 1830, of pulmonary disease, at the early age of thirty-seven.

Edinburgh
March, 1838

CHAPTER 1

My Early Life

I was born in Glasgow: my father held a situation in a mercantile house, that enabled him to keep his family respectable. I was the only surviving child, and no expense would have been spared on my education, had I been wise enough to appreciate the value of it; but, unfortunately for me, that was not the case. I had early learned to read; but novels, romances, and fairy tales, were my favourite books, and soon superseded all other kinds of reading. By this means, my ideas of life were warped from reality, and the world I had pictured in my imagination was very unlike the one in which I lived. The sober realities of life became tiresome and tasteless. Still panting after something unattainable, I became displeased with my situation in life, and neglected my education—not because I disliked it; on the contrary, I was fond of learning, and used to form very feasible plans of study, wherein I omitted nothing that was necessary to form the accomplished gentleman. I could pleasingly, in imagination, skim over the whole course of literature, and contemplate my future fame and wealth as the result; but when I considered how many years of arduous application would be required, I was too impatient to put it into practice. I had acquired too great a facility in raising castles in the air, and embellishing them with my fancy, to submit to the drudgery of building on a more stable foundation. Thus, straining at shadows, I lost substantial good.

Amongst other books which fell into my hands, when very young, was *Robinson Crusoe*. It was a great favourite; and at that time I believe I would willingly have suffered shipwreck, to be cast on an island like his. An island to one's self, I thought, what a happiness! and I have dreamed for hours together, on what I would do in such a situation. I have often played truant to wander into the fields, and read my favourite books; and, when I was not reading, my mind was perfectly bewildered with the romantic notions I had formed. Often have I travelled eagerly to the summit of some neighbouring hill, where the clouds seemed to mark the limits of the world I lived in, my mind filled with an indescribable expectation that I would there meet with something to realize my wild ideas, some enchanted scene or other; and when I reached its summit, and found those expectations disappointed, still the next similar place had the same attraction. The sky, with the ever-varying figures of the clouds, was an inexhaustible field for my imagination to work in; and the sea, particularly those views of it where the land could not be seen from the shore, raised indescribable feelings in my breast. The vessels leaving the coast, thought I, must contain happy souls; for they are going far away—all my fancied happy worlds were there. Oh, I thought, if I could 'once pass that blue line that separates the ocean and the sky!—then should I be content; for it seems the only barrier between me and happiness.

I was often beat for being absent from school, and urged to tell the cause. The reason I felt, but could not describe; and, the same fault recurring again and again, I was at last set down as incorrigible. What most surprised my friends was, that I never had any companions in my rambles; but a companion would have spoiled all my visions. Never did I enjoy so pure unmixed delight, as in those excursions: I feel not now, as I then did, the novelty of life and nature; but memory cherishes with fondness her first-born feelings, and I regret that those happy days are gone forever.

So ill exchanged for riper times,
To feel the follies and the crimes,
Of others or my own.

In some old romances which I had read, the life of a shepherd was described in colours so glowing, that I became quite enamoured of it, and would not give my parents rest until they procured such a situation for me. It was in vain that they assured me I would find everything different in that life from what I imagined. I could not believe it. They made some agreement with a farmer, from whom they got their milk and butter, to take me out with him to his farm, that I might learn the truth by experience. I set off with him on his buttermilk cart, my mind filled with the most extravagant anticipations of my new employment, and arrived at the farmer's house at night. Next morning I was called up at four o'clock to my new avocation, and an old man was sent out with me to show me my charge. I was left by him on a bleak hill, with fourscore sheep, and told that my breakfast and dinner would be brought out to me. I sat down to contemplate the scene: there were no sylvan groves, no purling streams, no shepherds piping in the dale—nothing but peat-bog was to be seen for miles around; the low scathed hills which reared their heads above the blackened soil were covered with heather, which still retained its winter suit; the shepherds had none of the appendages attributed to them in poetry or romance—they had neither pipe nor crook, and shepherdesses there were none. I tried to transform the female servant, who was in my master's house, into a shepherdess; but it would not do. It was a horrible caricature; she was a strong, masculine-looking Highland girl, anything but lovely or romantic. Surely, thought I, there must be some mistake here. I never spent a day so lonely and tiresome. My flock seemed to think they had got a fool to deal with, for they ran in every direction but the right one. It is true I had a dog, but he did not understand my language. We had not been long enough acquainted; and, by the time night came, I was pretty well convinced that the life of a shepherd was not what I had imagined it. Day after day passed without realizing any of my expectations. My feet got sore running through the rough heather; and I returned to my parents about a month after, completely cured of my predilection for a shepherd's life. One would think that this disappointment would have rendered me more cautious in forming opinions from the same source—but no! Indeed, it was ever my misfortune to pay dearly for my experience, and to profit little by that of others.

CHAPTER 2

Off to Sea

I found few boys of my own age who entered into my notions. One, indeed, I did find equally extravagant, and we were scarcely ever separate. Tired of living under the control of our parents, we determined to make a bold push at independence. We mustered as much money as bought the sixteenth of a lottery ticket. In the interval between buying and drawing—how we did dream! It never entered our minds that we would get less than the share of a prize of 30,000*l* and, of course, the disposal of the cash was the constant theme of our conversation. At last the wished-for day arrived, on which we were to receive intelligence of the fate of our ticket. We did not go to inquire concerning it until night. With hearts fluttering with apprehension we went to the shop where we had bought it. I would not go in, but sent in my companion. I durst scarcely look after him. To such an intense pitch of interest was my mind wrought up, that the criminal on his trial for some capital crime could not wait with more dreadful anxiety for the verdict of the jury, than I did for my companion to come out. He did come, but I was afraid to look him in the face, lest I should read disappointment in it. I waited for him to speak, but his tongue refused its office. I at last ventured to look in his face, and there I read the truth. Had he spoken and told me it was a blank, I might have doubted him, and thought he only joked me; but I could never doubt the expression of despair which I saw there depicted. Not a word was exchanged;

we walked on in stupefied vexation. After wandering about for some time unconscious of where we were going, he at last burst into tears. I could have willingly joined him, but I suspected that something else preyed on his mind. On asking him what distressed him so much, he said that part of the money with which he had purchased his share of the lottery ticket was the balance of an account, due to his father, which he had received without his knowledge. He depended on the receipt of his prize to pay it with interest, but now those hopes were blasted; he could never face home—his countenance would betray him, and his father was very severe.

He said he was determined to go to Greenock, and engage with some merchant vessel bound to Surinam. He had an uncle a planter there, and, of course, when he should arrive, there would be no danger of him; his uncle would procure his discharge from the ship, and the result, that he would become a gentleman. I listened eagerly to this. We had often expatiated on the pleasure of seeing foreign countries, and I resolved to accompany him, not doubting but his uncle would provide for me also, for his sake. Anything like adventure was always welcome to me, and my mind was soon decided.

We had no money, however, to carry us to Greenock; but I recollected a person who owed my father money, and I proposed to go and ask it in my father's name. This was the first time I had ventured to do anything so glaringly dishonest, and I hesitated long. I passed the door a dozen times before I mustered effrontery enough to go in; but it was drawing near the hour of shutting up, and I was obliged to resolve. I went in and asked the money. The candle burned dimly, and I stood as much in the shade as possible, but I am sure he noticed my embarrassment. However, he gave the money, and we hurried out of the town immediately.

We travelled all night, and next morning arrived in Greenock. After getting some breakfast, and brushing ourselves up a little, although we were very tired, we resolved on looking out for a vessel. On inquiry, we learned that there was no vessel in the harbour bound for Surinam. This was a disappointment; but, we thought, if we were once in the West Indies, we would find little difficulty in getting to the desired spot.

The first vessel we came to was a ship bound for Kingston, Jamaica. We went on board; and, inquiring for the captain, asked if he wanted any men. He looked at as with a smile of contempt, eyeing us from head to foot, "Men," said he, laying a particular emphasis on the word, (for neither of us exceeded thirteen years of age,) "it would be a pretty vessel that would be manned with *such men as you*—Whaur hae ye come frae na? Ye'll be some runawa weaver callans frae Glasgow, I'se warrant ye; but ye had better gang hame again, for I'm thinkin' ye'll like the sea waur than the loom." We were galled by his reply; but consoled ourselves with the idea that someone else would be glad to get us.

After trying several other vessels with nearly the same success, at last, tired and crestfallen, we were going home to our lodging, when an old man, who had seen us going from one vessel to another, accosted us, and asked if we wanted a ship. Replying in the affirmative, "you need not want that long," said he, "for if you go with me, I will soon find one for you. Where do you wish to go?"

"To Surinam."

"Then, you could not have come in a better time, for there is a vessel lying in the roads ready to sail for that place."

"Do you think they will take us?" said we. "Oh, to be sure they will, and glad to get you. I'll take you on board now if you like."

We assented, and he went to procure a boat to take us on board.

When he was gone, a sailor, who was standing by, and saw us talking to the old man, came up, and asked us what he had been saying. Having told him, he said the sooner we were off out of that the better; for the fellow who had been talking to us, was one of a set of rascals in pay of the press-gang; and that, instead of putting us on board of a vessel such as he described, he would put us on board the Tender; and that there was actually no such vessel in the roads as the one he had mentioned. We lost no time in taking his advice, and hurried home to our lodgings.

When there, my spirits began to sink; and the thought of how I had left my parents, and the distress they must be in about me, completely overcame me, and I burst into tears; and my companion feeling as bad as myself, we resolved to return home, and ask forgiveness of our parents; but, being fatigued with travelling, we put off our return until next morning.

When we got up next day our minds had recovered some of their former elasticity, and we felt less disposed to return than we did the preceding evening. The idea of the ridicule which we should have to encounter from our acquaintance, and, on my part, the stigma which would be thrown on my character for drawing the money in my father's name, seemed to be insurmountable barriers in the way, so we walked into the town with our minds still undecided.

In crossing the main street, we met one of our old schoolfellows, who had run away from his parents about six months before. He had just returned from the West Indies; and having leave for a few days to go to Glasgow to see his friends, he had got himself rigged out in the jolly-tar style—his jacket and trousers of fine blue cloth, white stockings, short-quartered shoes, a black silk handkerchief tied loosely round his neck, over which the collar of his checked shirt was folded neatly down—a glazed hat on his head, and an enormous quid of tobacco in his cheek. In fact, he was so completely metamorphosed, that we scarcely knew him; for when at school, he was remarked for being a soft, dull sort of boy.

On seeing us, he seized a hand of each, and exclaimed, "Oh, my eyes! Joe and Bill! how are ye, my hearties? what has brought you to Greenock: be ye looking out for a berth?" We were expressing our pleasure at having met him, when he said, "Don't be standing here in the street. Let's go and get a glass of grog." We remarked, that it would look very odd for boys like us to go into a tavern and call for liquor; but Tom thought that a very foolish objection, and leading the way into a tavern, we followed him. As he walked in before us, I perceived that he had altered his manner of walking quite to the rocking gait of the veteran tar. I certainly thought that Tom had been an apt scholar; he seemed to be as finished a sailor as if he had been twenty years at sea. From being a boy of few words, he had acquired a surprising volubility of tongue, along with an affected English accent. He could curse and swear, chew tobacco and drink grog; and although we perceived much affectation in what Tom said and did, still we were disposed to think him a very clever fellow. When seated over our grog, we disclosed our minds to him, and inquired if he could assist us in getting a vessel. Tom looked rather grave on this subject, and sinking his voice from the high English accent he had acquired so rapidly, said he was not sure whether he could get a vessel for us or not; " but," said he, " in the mean time drink your grog, and we will see about that after."

Warmed by the liquor, Tom began and gave us an account of his voyage, which, as he afterwards owned, he painted in very extravagant colours. We were so charmed with his description, that we gave up all idea of going home, and adjourned from the tavern to Tom's lodgings, where he displayed to our wondering eyes the treasures he had acquired by his West India voyage—conch-shells, cocoa-nuts, and stalks of Indian corn, which were designed to grace his mother's chimney-piece, and excite the wonder of her visitors.

Between the liquor we had drunk, and what we had heard and seen, we were in high spirits, and went out to perambulate the town; but, going up the main street, towards the head inn, I met my father full in the face. He had just arrived from Glasgow in search of us. I thought I would have sunk into the earth. Confounded and ashamed, I stood like a felon caught in some depredation. Tom ran off, and left William and I to manage affairs as we could. My father was the first who broke silence. "Well, Joseph," said he, " will you tell me the meaning of this jaunt you have taken? But I am going to Mr. C——'s, and you had better come with me, and we shall talk over the matter there."

We followed him without saying a word, and when we were seated in Mr. C———'s, he again asked my motive for leaving home. I looked in William's face, and saw he was determined. I then said we were resolved on going to sea, and that we had come to Greenock for that purpose.

Mr. C and my father said everything they could to dissuade us from our foolish resolution, but to little purpose. The idea of the ridicule we would have to bear from our acquaintance if we returned, and Tom's exaggerated description of the pleasures of a sea life, had confirmed us in our determination.

"Well," said my father (after he had reasoned the matter with me, and painted what a sailor's life was in reality, with little effect,) "I might exert the right I have over you, as a parent, in forcing you to return, but I will not. If you have so far forgot your duty to me, and to yourself, after all that I have done for you, as to throw yourself away as a common ship-boy, where you can have no opportunity of learning anything but wicked, ness, you may do it, but remember my words—you will repent it, when you will perhaps have no father to question the propriety of your conduct. Indeed, after the dishonest action you have been guilty of at home, I don't know but your presence would be more disagreeable to me than your absence, unless you altered much for the better; and if I have any very anxious wish that you would return, it is more on your poor mother's account than my own. Oh, how could you leave us in the manner you did, without a cause?—The first night you were absent from home, your mother was frantic. She wandered from place to place in search of you—and was sure you were not in life—that some accident had befallen you. When she knows the truth, how cruel must she think you?—O! Joseph, after all our care and attention, I am afraid you will bring down our grey hairs with sorrow to the grave."

Here the tears came into my father's eyes, and his voice became choked. I could bear it no longer, and burst into tears. My first impulse was to throw myself at his feet, and beg forgiveness; but the obstacles which were in the way of my return before, again recurring to my mind, prevented me, and I only wept in sullen silence.

"Say no more to him now," said Mr. C. "Give him until to-morrow to think on what you have said; and if he be then of the same opinion, we shall procure a good ship for him, and see him properly fitted out." My lather took his advice, and did not resume the subject that day. He wrote, however, to William's father, telling where his son was.

Next morning he arrived, and insisted on taking him home by force, and even beat and abused him in the house we were in; but my father and Mr. C. interfered, and represented to him how foolish his conduct was, as he might be sure the boy would take the first opportunity of running away again. He was at last brought to reason, and agreed to be guided by my father. We were again asked what we had determined on doing, and I re-plied that we were fixed in our determination of going to sea.

It was then proposed to get us bound immediately, as my father could not be spared from his business, and was obliged to return next day. Mr. C. took us to a friend of his, a Mr. G., a respectable merchant and ship-owner, who was in want of apprentices at that time for some of his vessels. We were there bound for three years, and attached to a letter-of-marque brig, which carried eighteen guns, loading at that time for New Providence.

The afternoon was spent in purchasing the necessary articles to fit me out. When that was finished, my father, feeling uneasy on my mother's account, resolved to return to Glasgow that night. Before going away, he said, "I could almost wish your mother saw you before you went away—and yet, perhaps it would be better that she would not. You will soon find yourself among very strange company; and if I am not wrong informed, company from whom you will be able to learn little that is good; but I trust you will remember the religious instruction you have received from your parents, when you are far from them; and although you have grieved and disobeyed your earthly parents, I hope you will not forget your Creator. Remember his eye is on you wherever you go; and although you may be bereft of every other stay, still he will be ever with you, to succour, and to help, if you call upon him. Farewell, my boy, God help you!"

My heart sunk within me. As the coach started, I saw him wipe the tears from his eyes. I must surely be a hardened wretch, thought I, to persist so resolutely in what I know to be wrong, and what is breaking the heart of my parents; but I was roused from my reflections by someone slapping me on the shoulder. It was Tom—"Well, my boys, so you have got bound to our owner—have you?"

"Do you belong to Mr. G. also?" said I.

"To be sure, and I don't think but I shall get into your ship too, although she sails so soon; for I don't like the one I am in."

We felt well pleased that Tom was to be our shipmate; and in the contemplation of all the good fortune that I thought awaited me, I am ashamed to say, that I nearly forgot my distressed parents.

As for William, the moment his father set off (for my father and his went up to Glasgow together), the poor fellow seemed quite relieved! His mother had died when he was very young, and his father being a man of a morose, severe disposition, he scarcely knew what parental tenderness was. How different from me! He had some excuse for what he had done; but I had none.

Tom went up to Glasgow next day, to see his friends; and a day or two after, William and I were sent on board, to commence our seamanship. The first day or two passed away well enough. There was little or nothing to do. The third day, the mate called us aft to the quarter-deck.

"Do you see that flag?" said he, pointing to the mast-head. It had got entangled in the signal halliards. "Now let me see which of you will get up first and clear it."

Will and I got on the shrouds, and mounted with great alacrity, until we got to that part of the shrouds which takes a sweep outwards to meet the edge of the top. Will was up over it in a twinkling; for he had been used to mount the rigging of the vessels at the Broomielaw; but I thought it a dangerous-looking place, and seeing a hole through the top, by the side of the mast,

I proceeded to squeeze myself through it; which being an offence against the laws of good seamanship (as the sailors' name for it denotes, being called the *lubber's hole*), the mate seized a rope's end on deck, and running up the shrouds after me, called out, "You young dog! is that the way you are taking?"

I made haste to rectify my error by taking the same route that Will had pursued; but, in my hurry, from the fear of the rope's end, when I reached the edge of the top, I let go the hold with my feet, and being suspended by my hands, would soon have dropped on the deck, or into the sea, had the mate not caught hold, and assisted me up. Will had by this time got as far as the crosstrees; but he was foiled in his attempts to climb up the royal-mast. The mate, however, thought we had done enough for once, and we were ordered down; but our exercise at this kind of work being continued every day while in harbour, we soon became expert at it.

CHAPTER 3
Life on Board Ship

At last, the long-expected day of sailing arrived, and among the first of the men who came on board was Tom. He had received liberty to join our ship, and, men and boys, we mustered about sixty hands. The greater number, when they came on board, were " half-seas-over," and the ship was in great confusion.

Towards evening, it began to blow fresh, and I became miserably sick. No one took any notice of me, unless when I went to the weather-side of the vessel to vomit, when someone or other of my tender-hearted shipmates would give me a kick or a push, and, with an oath, bid me go to leeward.

In this state, I was knocked about, from one place to another, until at last I lay down in the waist of the vessel, on the lee-side, with my head opposite to one of the scuppers.[1] I had not been long there, when someone came running to the side. I looked up to see who it was, and saw poor Tom in nearly as bad a plight as myself. I was too sick to speak to him, or I would have asked why he had omitted this in his description of the pleasures of a sea life.

I had not seen William from the time I became sick, but at that time I could feel interested for no one, or about anything. I only wished I were on shore, and nothing should ever tempt me to put my foot on board of a vessel again.

Night came on, and the weather being cold, I began to wish that I could get below. I crawled to the first hatchway I could find, which happened to be the steerage. As this place was ap-

---

1. Scuppers, the holes by which the water runs off the deck.

propriated to the petty officers of the ship, and they being all employed on deck, I was allowed to get down unmolested. There were some of the cables coiled in the steerage; and as I had experienced the inconvenience of being in the way, I crept in as far as I could, beyond the cables, where some old sails were lying, and there, although not relieved from sickness, I was at least free from annoyance.

I had not been long there, when the steerage mess came down to supper; and I quaked with terror when I heard the gunner say, "I wonder where all those boys are. I can't get one of them to do either one thing or another."

"They'll be stowed away in some hole or other, I'll warrant ye," said the boatswain, "but if I had hold of them, I would let them feel the weight of a rope's end."

I strove to keep in my breath lest they should hear me, but at the moment my stomach heaved, and in spite of all my efforts to suppress it, I made such a noise that I was overheard.

"Who the devil's that?" cried the boatswain; "someone of the rascals stowed away in the cable tier—hold the lantern, and I'll haul him out whoever he is."

Already I thought I felt the rope's end on my shoulders, when I was unexpectedly relieved from my apprehensions, by the mate calling them on deck to arrange the watches for the night. While they were gone, I squeezed myself in behind some boxes, where I was pretty sure they could not get at me. When they came down again, they had forgotten the circumstance; and those whose watch was below got into their hammocks.

A little before daylight, I felt inclined to go on deck, as I was nearly suffocated in my hiding place, and slipping out cautiously, got up the ladder without disturbing any of them. I had felt pretty well settled, when my head was down; but whenever I got up, the sickness returned, and my stomach being completely empty, my efforts were most distressing. An old sailor who was standing near me advised me to take a drink of salt water. I thought it was a rough cure; I tried it, however, but it was no sooner down than up again.

"Take another drink," said he; I did so—the same result followed. He advised me to take a third.

"Oh, no," said I, "I can take no more." I then leaned over the lee bow of the vessel; and whether it was the fresh air or the salt water I know not, but I soon got better; and in the course of an hour or two I began to move about pretty briskly.

While I was stirring about, the carpenter came forward to me and inquired if I was sick. "No," I said.

"Will you have any objection to attend our mess?"

"I don't know, what have I to do?"

"Only draw our provision, and boil our kettle morning and evening."

"Very well—I am willing."

He took me down to the steerage, and showed me where things lay. When breakfast-time came I got their kettle boiled, and brought down their mess of *bargoo*, and sat down to take my breakfast with them; but before I had taken half-a-dozen spoonfuls, it began to discompose my stomach; and getting up to pass them for the deck, the motion of rising brought the contents of my stomach up to my mouth. I endeavoured to keep it down, but was obliged to give it vent, and it flew like water from a fire engine over the mess. The boatswain, who was a surly old fellow, and who had been the principal sufferer, rose up in a fury, and seizing the wooden dish that held the *bargoo*, threw it at my head. I escaped the blow of the dish, but the contents came right on my face and blinded me. I tried to grope my way up the ladder, but they did not give me time to get up, for they threw me out of the hatchway. When I got to my feet the whole of the seamen on deck gathered round, and began to jeer me on my appearance; but I managed to flounder on through them to the head, where I got some water and washed myself. Ah! thought I, this is hard usage; yet I could scarcely refrain from laughing at the idea of spoiling their mess.

I walked about the deck for some time, ruminating on my folly in exchanging my comfortable home for a place like this. Towards dinner-time, the carpenter came and asked me to prepare the mess-dishes for dinner, but I told him he might find someone else, for I would not do it.

"The more fool you are," said he, "you will soon find yourself worse off."

I was then obliged to shift my things into the forecastle amongst the crew. Here I found William lying in one of the berths, so sick that he could not lift his head. When he saw me he beckoned me to him. "O Joseph," said he, " this is misery. I wish we were at home again; but I will never live to return."

"No fear of that," I said, "I was as sick as you are, and I am now nearly well."

At this moment the vessel gave a heave, and down I came on the deck. William began to make cascades, and I was soon as bad as ever, and got tumbled into the berth beside him. Shortly after, the seamen's dinner was brought down, and having served themselves, one of them called out, " You green-horns, in there, will you have some beef and biscuit?"

"No, no," said I, "but if you will be kind enough to open my chest, you will find a cake of gingerbread in it—I will thank you to hand it to me."

While he was searching for the gingerbread, he cast his eyes on a large case bottle, filled with whiskey, which Mr. C. had given me when I parted with him. He immediately gave up his search for the gingerbread, and hauling out the bottle and holding it up, he cried, "D—n my eyes, messmates, if I ha'n't found a prize."

"Here with it," cried a dozen voices at once, and in spite of my remonstrances, they deliberately handed it round until there was not above a glass left.

"Oh shame," said one of them, "give the boy a drop of his own grog;" but I could not look at it—the smell was sickening.

"No, no," said I, "send that after the rest."

"Right," said one of them, "boys have no use for grog."

"Will you give me the gingerbread now?" said I.

"Oh, by the by, I had forgot that; here it is for you, my hearty."

The most of them went on deck, and left William and I to reflect on the justice of their appropriation of my property. However, the liquor was a thing I cared little about, and it gave me
the less uneasiness. We were now allowed to lie quietly enough
until night, when those whose watch was below came down to
go to bed—one of them came to the berth where William and I
were lying, and seizing him by the neck, cried out, "Hello, who
the devil's this in my berth?"

"It is two of the Johnnie-raws that are sick," replied one of
them.

"Johnnie-raw or Johnnie-roasted, they must get out of that,
for I want to turn in."

Out we were bundled, and during the whole course of that
night we were knocked about from one place to another, by
each succeeding watch.

Next morning early, the word was passed for the boys to go
aft to the quarter-deck. It was hard rooting them out; but at last
we were mustered—six in all. When we were assembled, the
mate addressing us, said, "I think I have given you long enough
time to recover from your sickness. You, Tom, have no right to
be sick. You were at sea before."

I looked at Tom: there was not a more miserable-looking object amongst us. I could scarcely allow myself to believe that he
was the same being whom we saw swaggering on the streets of
Greenock a few days before. We were then appointed to different
watches. William and I were luckily appointed to the same one,
which being on duty at the time, we were ordered to scrub the
hen-coops, and feed the fowls, while the men washed the deck.
The boys were always made the drudges in everything dirty and
disagreeable. But the duty of the ship was little in comparison to
the way in which we were teased and ill used by the sailors.

I have often been roused up after a fatiguing watch, and just
when I had fallen into a profound sleep, to go and fetch a drink
of water for some of the crew. A fellow, of the name of Donald
McMillan, was one of our chief tormentors. He used to invent
new mortifications for us; and he was of so brutal and savage a

disposition, that he would beat and abuse the boys for the most trifling fault, and often without cause. I am sure, if the conduct of the men had been reported to the captain, he would not have allowed the boys to be used in the manner they were. But we were afraid to say anything concerning our usage, knowing that they could find numberless methods of tormenting without openly beating us, I began, however, to get used to the sea; and taking courage, I strove to get through as well as I could. It was, nevertheless, with a great effort that I could prevent my spirits from sinking under the many hardships and contumely I had to endure. Nothing but the hope of leaving the vessel when she returned home kept me alive. Poor William lost all heart; he became melancholy and moping, and used to cry for hours together, when we were on watch at night. In this state he was ill calculated for the duty he had to perform, and was brow-beaten by almost everyone in the ship. This sunk his naturally buoyant spirits; and at length he became so accustomed to ill usage, that he seemed afraid I would also turn against him. I, however, had known him in happier days; but his feelings were morbidly acute, and little calculated to struggle through the ill usage which a ship apprentice had to endure.

As we proceeded on our voyage, the weather became delight-ful; and getting into the trade-winds, we got on so pleasantly, often for days together, without changing a sail, that had we not been tormented by the seamen, we would have been compara-tively comfortable. But the only happy periods I enjoyed were, when my turn came to look-out aloft—seated on the crosstrees, away from the din of the deck, with the clear blue sky above, and the sea extending far as the eye could reach beneath. It was there I almost realized some of the fairy scenes I had pictured in my imagination. I felt myself in an enchanted world of my own, and would sit watching the clouds as they passed along, comparing their shape to some romantic image in my mind, and peopling them with corresponding inhabitants.

So lost was I in those reveries that I did not feel the time passing; and when the man came up to relieve me, I have often volunteered to stop his two hours also. When I came down on deck, I felt as it were cast from heaven to earth, and used to long for my turn to look-out again. These were the only pleasures I enjoyed unmolested and unenvied; for few of my comrades required any pressing to allow me to remain in their place. The nights were now delightful; the moon shone in "cloudless majesty," and the air was so cool and pleasant, that it was preferred by the seamen to the day; instead of going below, they often gathered in knots on the deck, and played at various games, or told stories. Many of them were good at this. One of them, a Swede, had as large a collection as any person I ever knew: they were those of his country—mostly terrific—ghosts and men possessed of supernatural powers, were the heroes of his stories. The flying Dutchman, and many other naval apparitions, were talked of and descanted on with much gravity. Sailors, in general, are very superstitious, and these stories were listened to with the greatest attention.

One of the stories he narrated was of a seaman with whom his father had sailed. He was a wonderful fellow: he could arrest a ship in full sail. When he wanted liquor, he had nothing to do but bore a hole in the mast, and out flowed rum, brandy, or any liquor he wished for. He once had committed some crime, for which he was sentenced to be flogged; the crew were assembled, and the culprit stripped and tied up; the boatswain raised his brawny arm to give the lash, but by some invisible power his arm was arrested in the air, and he stood with it stretched out, unable to bring it down. The master-at-arms raised his cane to strike the boatswain for his seeming neglect of duty, and his arm was arrested in like manner. The captain, enraged to see both boatswain and master-at-arms in the strange position, drew his sword, and raised it, to let it fall on some of their heads, when he shared the same fate. Thus all three stood with their arms upraised in air; nor would our hero release them from their awkward position, until he was pardoned and taken down. Some time after, he committed another crime; but they were afraid his power was too potent on board for them to proceed against him there: therefore he was conveyed ashore, and tried. In addition to the alleged crime, they brought forward a charge of dealing with the devil. The proof was reckoned conclusive, and he was sentenced to suffer death. He gave himself no uneasiness about it. The day arrived on which he was to be executed; and the guard entered his prison for the purpose of conveying him to the place of execution. When they entered, he was busily drawing a ship upon the wall with chalk; he requested them to wait a moment until he would finish it. They did so. When he had done, he bade those about him *adieu*; and lifting his foot, as if it were to step into his mimic ship, he disappeared from their eyes in a moment, and was never heard of after.

One night the weather was hazy, when I was appointed to look out ahead along with an old sailor, who was remarkable for being an attentive listener when any stories were telling. The moon was up; but a dense curtain of clouds hid her almost completely from our view. The wind came in gusts, and swept the clouds along in irregular masses. Sometimes a doubtful light would be thrown around us; again a dark cloud would intervene, and we could scarcely see the end of the jib-boom. The wind whistled through the rigging of the vessel occasionally with a low murmuring sound; then it would rise gradually to such a fury, that we could scarcely hear each other talk. We were anxiously looking out, when he asked me if I did not see something like a sail ahead. I replied that I did not. He pointed to the place where he imagined he saw it. I looked again. A partial gleam of light, occasioned by a cloud of lighter texture passing over the moon, being thrown on the place, I really thought I saw something like a sail. He did not wait for any more investigation, but gave the alarm. The mate came forward to see it; but the light was so uncertain, that he could not decide on what it was. The watch gathered about the bows of the vessel, everyone having something to say on the subject. One pretended he saw a sail plainly—she was a square-rigged vessel, with all her sails set; another said she was schooner-rigged. Ominous whispers now began to go round, intimating that her appearance was anything but natural. The mate hearing some hints that were dropped, said, "There was a cursed deal too much of that ghost story-telling of late; and he would lay his head to a marlinspike, that this would turn out to be no sail after all."

At this moment (luckily for his prediction) the moon broke through in all her splendour; and as far as the eye could reach, not a speck on the surface of the dark blue waters could be traced. The laugh was now turned against those who had pretended to see the sail; but they only shook their heads doubtfully, and wished that nothing bad might follow. I venture to say that everyone on board joined in that wish.

CHAPTER 4

I Return to Scotland

A few days after that, we fell in with a vessel which we hailed, and found she was bound for Greenock from Jamaica. She brought to; and all those who wished to send letters to their friends were ordered to make haste and write them. I got out my writing materials; but I was at a loss what to say. Had I been inclined to tell the truth, I would have been at no loss; but I could not bear the idea of owning how grossly I had been deceived in my ideas of a sailor's life. However, I believe I gave them room to think that I did not like it very well. I had lost so much time in resolving what to write, that the letters were called for before I had time to give any particulars. When I was sealing my letter, I ardently wished I could insinuate myself inside of it.

Nothing particular occurred during the rest of our voyage, until a few days before we made the land. One morning early a sail appeared to windward. The captain, looking at her through his telescope, was of opinion that she was a French privateer. All hands were called to quarters; and as she bore down upon us, the captain's opinion was confirmed, for she fired a gun and hoisted French colours. We were well manned, and carried as many guns as she appeared to do. Everything was prepared for action; only the guns were not run out, and the ports were down. The captain had ordered all the men, with the exception of the petty officers, to lie down on the deck, concealed behind the bulwarks, until he should give the word of command. She was bearing fast down upon us, when I was ordered to the magazine to hand up ammunition. I was frightened enough when on deck; but when below, I became much more so. It was not long before a broadside was fired. I was sure it was from the enemy, and, stunned with the noise, fell flat on my face. "God be merciful to me!" said I; for I was sure we were going to the bottom.

In a minute after, I was surprised with the men cheering on deck. I mounted the ladder; and venturing my head up the hatchway, saw the strange ship a good way to leeward, making all the sail she could. On inquiring, I found that she had borne down close on us, thinking we were an unarmed merchant ship, and ordered us to strike. The reply we gave him was what had alarmed me so much; for our men, starting to their feet on the word of command from the captain, ran out the guns, and gave her a broadside. She was so completely taken in by the reception she met with, that she sheered off without firing a shot. The captain's orders were, not to deviate from his course, else we might have captured her.

We now drew near the land, and the lead was frequently hove to ascertain what sort of a bottom we had.[1] Pieces of sugar-cane, melons, and fruit of various kinds, were floating about; birds in great numbers hovered about the ship; and everything intimated that the land was nigh. It was my turn to look out aloft, and I felt sure of the bottle of rum which is usually given to the man who espies land first. I was not long up, when I thought I saw land off the lee bow. I watched it attentively. It became better defined every minute. I was positive it was land, and I sung out, "Land, ho!" with a joyous voice.

The intelligence ran through the crew; and I saw them skipping about on deck, seemingly delighted with the news. The mate came up beside me to see where the land lay. I pointed it out to him; but it soon altered its appearance, and began slowly to move up from the verge of the horizon, and in less than ten minutes not a vestige of the appearance remained. To me it

---

1. There is a cavity in the bottom of the lead, which is filled with tallow, to which sand or gravel, composing the bed of the sea, adheres.

looked like enchantment; but I learned from the mate that such sights were not uncommon, and were termed by the seamen, "Cape Flyaway."

In the course of the day we made the real land, but were too late to get into the harbour that night. However, next morning early we got in, and came to anchor nearly opposite Fort Charlotte, town of Nassau, after a passage of six weeks. As we entered the harbour, we found a sloop-of-war lying there; and some of our men, afraid of being pressed, took a boat, and made towards the shore; but the officers of the man-of-war observing them, they sent a boat in pursuit. Our fellows pulled hard, and would have made the shore before them, had they not fired a musket-shot or two, and obliged them to lie-to. They were then all taken on board the sloop-of-war; but in the course of the day they were sent back, with the exception of Donald McMillan, who had given some insolence to the officers; and they sent word that they had kept him to teach him better manners. The boys did not mourn much at his detention, nor, I believe, did any of the crew; for his disposition was such, that everyone hated him.

We were not long at anchor before we were surrounded by canoes from the shore, with black fellows in them, selling fruits of various kinds, not common in Britain. Here we got rid of some of our money, in exchange for bananas, guavas, and pineapples; and I almost forgot all my sufferings in the novelty of the scene around me. The white sandy beach, the light ornamented wooden buildings, walks bordered by palm and cocoanut-trees, with the singular dresses of the planters and their negroes, were objects which made me think myself in a new world. In the course of the day we got off fresh beef and plenty of vegetables, which was a treat, having had nothing but salt provision from the time of leaving Greenock; and to complete our happiness, we got an extra allowance of rum sent from the owners of the cargo.

Next day we began to deliver the cargo. There was no quay, but wharfs here and there to the different stores. When the tide was in, we got our boats unloaded by means of a crane; but at low water we were obliged to push the hogsheads from the boats into the sea, and wading up to the middle to roll them out before us to the shore. This was most fatiguing and disagreeable work; therefore we were not sorry when it was finished. On Sundays, (the negroes' market-day in the West Indies,) the half of the crew alternately got leave to go ashore. William and I happened to be of the first party, and we were delighted with everything around us; but we could not discover that the inhabitants were disposed to give their money away for nothing any more than at home. Nor could we find anything to justify the notion, that a rapid fortune could be acquired there, without similar exertion to that we had been accustomed to see in other places. After taking a view of the town, and purchasing some shells and other curiosities, we came on board well pleased with the holiday we had had on shore. Soon after this, we began to take in our cargo, which consisted principally of rum, cotton, and coffee.

As yet it had been delightful weather, only excessively warm in the middle of the day; but the mornings and evenings were very pleasant. The third morning, after we began to take in our cargo, came on sultry and close. The air was oppressive—the clouds hung low and heavy, and ere long the rain burst out in torrents. This had not continued ten minutes, until we were up to our knees in water on the deck. It poured down so fast that it could not escape by the scuppers. The earth seemed threatened with another deluge. The whole face of the heavens was dark as night. The crew were all employed in striking the top-gallant masts, lowering the yards, and making everything snug.

"This is shocking rain!" said I to an old sailor who stood near me.

"Yes," said he; "but we will have worse than rain by and by."

He had scarcely said so, when the heavens seemed to open, and a flash of lightning burst forth, so strong and vivid that it took the sight from my eyes. A clap of thunder followed so loud and long, that it must have appalled the stoutest heart. Flash after flash succeeded each other, and the peals of thunder were incessant. I thought the last day was come. Heaven and earth seemed jumbled together in one mass of fire; and the continued noise of the thunder struck my imagination as the result of the fabric falling to ruin.

Towards the afternoon the wind blew with great fury. The vessels in the harbour began to drag their anchors, and before night many of them were on shore; but we were well moored, and did not stir. The storm continued the greater part of the night; and such a night I hope I will never see again. No one would go below. We did not know the moment the lightning might strike the vessel, and perhaps send her to the bottom. It is in vain for me to attempt to convey any adequate description of that dreadful night in words. No one can form an idea of its awfulness, unless he had seen it. The men stood huddled in groups, on the deck, in silence. Indeed it was useless to speak, for they could not be heard; nor scarcely could they see each other, unless when the lightning shot its awful glare athwart their faces, and made their horror visible for an instant; and the livid cadaverous colour it shed over their countenances, gave them an expression truly appalling.

About one o'clock in the morning the storm began to moderate: the flashes of lightning became weaker and less frequent; the awful roaring of the thunder changed into a hoarse growl, and at length died away. By two the storm had so much subsided, that the seamen, with the exception of the harbour watch, went below to their hammocks.

I was surprised next morning, when I got up at sunrise, to see no vestige of the night's storm remaining. All was calm and serene, save a pleasant breeze from the shore, which brought the most delicious odours along with it. The sun rose with unusual brightness, and all nature seemed renovated. We could not, indeed, have imagined that there had been a storm the preceding night, if the effects of its fury had not been visible in the roofless buildings and stranded vessels around us.

Our vessel had suffered little or no damage.

We got on with our loading, and in a short time we were ready for sea.

The day before we sailed, the owners sent a present of a bottle of rum to each man, to hold a sort of "chevo," as the sailors called it. The decks were cleared, and we sat down in groups with our bottles, and commenced drinking. All went on very well for a time. The song and joke went round, and harmony and good humour prevailed. But when the drink began to operate, some of them who had differences during the voyage began to "tell their minds." The result was, that they came to high words, and from that to blows. The rest of the crew took different sides, according as they were interested, and the deck soon became a scene of confusion and bloodshed. I had drunk little, and mounted into the foretop to be out of "harm's way;" and from thence saw the combat, without danger of getting any of the blows which were dealing out so plentifully. The mate came forward to try to quell the disturbance; but they knocked him over a kedge anchor that lay on the deck, and broke one of his ribs.

At length the disturbance died away, and I came down on deck. Some deep drinkers had gathered the bottles which had escaped destruction during the fight, and were emptying their contents. Others were lying insensibly drunk and vomiting. Broken bottles, with their contents promiscuously mixed on the deck with the blood of the combatants, lay scattered about in every direction. I never saw such miserable-looking wretches as they were next morning. Most of them were horrified. Almost all of them bore marks of the late fray—black eyes, swelled lips, sprained thumbs, &c. &c. As the vessel was to sail that day, the captain, in order to bring them about a little, served them out their grog, and they quickly got to rights again.

We got up our anchors, and set sail with a fair wind. I could not describe the emotions I felt when I saw the vessel's head turned homewards. I was all joyous anticipation of meeting with my parents. "I shall never leave them again," thought I. " I shall obey them in everything, and we shall be so happy. I have seen my folly, and I shall make a good use of my experience."

Nothing particular occurred on the passage home, until we

got near the British coast, when the weather became extremely cold. The look-out aloft was no longer a pleasant berth. I have often been so benumbed when the man came up to relieve me, that I could scarcely move my limbs to come down upon deck. The weather had been rough for some time, but one afternoon it began to blow uncommonly hard. The wind was fair, however, and the captain seemed unwilling to take in sail, but the gale increasing, he ordered the top-gallant sails to be handed. William and I, with another boy, went up to hand the main top-gallant sail. The vessel was pitching dreadfully. William went to the weather, and I went to the lee caring, to haul in the leach of the sail. The part which bound the yard to the mast gave way, and it pitched out with such violence, that William was shook from his hold, and precipitated into the sea. I got a dreadful shock.

This was an awful moment. Every pitch that the vessel gave, the yard was thrown out from the mast with such force, that it was a miracle I escaped. The other boy had got in on the mast, but it appeared impossible for me to follow him. Nothing could save me, unless the despairing hold that I retained, and I could not have kept it long, for every shock rendered me weaker; but some of the seamen were sent up with a loose line, and succeeded in bracing the yard to the mast, and I was relieved from my perilous situation.

Poor William! I saw him fall. "O God!" he cried, as he fell. I heard no more. The next moment he was swallowed by the waves. They told me he never rose. It was impossible to do anything to save him in such weather with any effect. His fate made a great impression on my mind, for he was my only companion. He was a clever boy, warm-hearted, and kind in his disposition, although he had become quite broken-hearted. Nor did he seem relieved from his melancholy by the prospect of returning home; for he was sure that his father would do nothing to get him free from the ship; and even if he did, he could feel little pleasure in the anticipation of his usage there.

"O Joseph!" he would often say, "if I had a father and mother like yours, how happy would I be! but I may truly say that I am an orphan! To be sure, while my mother was living, she was everything that was good and affectionate to me; but when she died, I lost the only friend I had in the world, for my father never was kind to me, and after he married again, I never had a happy minute in the house; and if I were to go home again, even supposing that he would get me free from the ship, things would be worse than before. But I am sure I will not live to return. There is a heavy something hangs on my mind, that tells me I will not see the end of this voyage; but I do not feel grieved at it, I rather feel a pleasure in the idea. Then I will be free from ill usage and persecution; and what makes me long for my death, is the hope that I will meet my mother in heaven, never to part from her again." I could not forbear weeping when he spoke in this manner; and I tried to cheer him as much as I could, by putting him in mind of our former schemes of happiness and fortune; but he only shook his head, and said, "This is not the world we dreamed it was; but even so, I have no friends, no prospects, and death appears to me to be the only thing that can alter my situation for the better." Poor fellow! he little thought it was so near.

The gale still continued to increase, and all our sails were taken in, with the exception of a close-reefed foretopsail. The wind veered about, and blew a hurricane. Some of the sails were torn in ribbons before they could be handed. The sea ran mountains high. The sky was darkened, and the flapping of the sails and rattling of the blocks made such a noise that we could scarcely hear our own voices. The sea broke over us in such a way that boats, spars, and camboose, were carried off the deck, and the helm became almost totally unmanageable, although four men were constantly at it. When a sea struck the vessel, she creaked as if her very sides were coming together. The men were obliged to lash themselves to every place where they could find safety, to prevent their being washed overboard; and in this manner we stood in awful suspense, waiting the issue of the storm. One minute she would rise perched, as it were, on the verge of a precipice; the next, she would descend through the yawning gulf as if she would strike the very bottom of the sea, while vivid flashes of lightning contributed to throw a horrible glare over the scene.

Three days were we tossed about in this manner, every day expecting it to be our last, for we thought it impossible that the ship could weather the gale. During that time we could not get below, the hatches being battened down, and we had to subsist on dry biscuit, or eat raw pork with it, for we could get nothing cooked.

On the fourth day the storm abated, and the weather cleared up; but the vessel rolled so that we expected her masts to go overboard. After the gale, we fell in with some vessels which had suffered severely; one in particular, had lost all her masts. We were at this time near the mouth of the Channel; and next day, we made Cape Clear. I could not express what I felt at again seeing the shores of Britain. My imagination was hard at work drawing pictures of the future. We ran up along the Irish coast with a fair wind, and at last came in sight of the well-known Craig of Ailsa; and passing it, the Cumbrays, and the Clough lighthouse, we anchored in Greenock Roads.

I was in transports of joy at the idea of getting home again; but a doubt would often cross my mind, whether my father might feel inclined to get me free from the vessel, after so obstinately persisting in going to sea; I, at least, felt sensible that I did not deserve such indulgence. The day after we arrived, however, my mind was set at ease, for my mother came from Glasgow to see me, and the first words she said, were, "Well, Joseph, are you tired of the sea?" The tears came into my eyes, but I could not speak. "I find you don't like it," said she: "you have found out, I believe, that your father's description of a sea life was a true one—well, we must try and get you home again."

A day or two afterwards, my father came to Greenock, and having settled matters with the owners, I went home with him on the coach, fully resolved that I should be more wise in future. I had a joyful meeting with my friends, and, for a time, all went on pleasantly; but my restless disposition still remained the same, and I soon grew tired of home. My parents expected a miraculous change in me; and when they found that my voyage had made me little wiser, any indiscretion was generally checked with an allusion to my former conduct. This irritated my feelings. Those boys who used to associate with me, now avoided my company; most of them, I believe, by the injunction of their parents.

There were two boys with whom I had been on the most friendly terms—their parents and mine were very intimate—they were constant playfellows of mine before I went to sea, and I had occasionally seen them after my return, without their seeming any way reserved towards me. Some months after I came home, however, I happened to be diverting myself with them in their courtyard; we were playing at hide-and-seek; having hid myself in the straw-house, I heard their father call them and ask who was with them; when they told him, he said, "Never let me see you in that boy's company again, for he ran away from his parents, and he may induce you to do the same."

This went like a dagger to my heart. It humbled me severely in my own eyes. I waited until he went into the house, and then slunk away like a felon. From that day I thought everyone who looked at me were passing similar observations in their minds. My temper became soured, and I grew melancholy and restless. I brooded continually over the indignity which I conceived I had suffered. "Then," said I to myself, "I have become an object of contempt to everyone. I can never endure this—I will not remain in Glasgow."

CHAPTER 5

Enlisted

One evening, in January, 1809, returning from dinner to school, brooding over my real or imaginary evils—my mind in such a state of despondency that I could almost have taken away my life—I determined to leave Glasgow, for, I thought, if once out of it, I should be happy. In this state of mind, walking down the High Street, I met a soldier. The thought struck me instantly that I would enlist, although I rather felt a prejudice against the army. Yet, by enlisting, I would get out of Glasgow, and to me that was every tiling. I followed the soldier, and asked him where his officer lodged. He showed me the place, and I enlisted, with the proviso that he would send me out of the town immediately.

I was sent to Paisley, and remained with the party there until the recruits were ordered to march for headquarters. When I came into Glasgow to join them, in passing through the Bridge-gate, I met my mother. I had never written to my parents, nor had they heard of me from the time I enlisted. I could scarcely define my feelings: shame—grief—a sort of sullen despair—a sense that I had cut myself off from the world—that I had done my worst, and a determination to push it to the utmost—were mingled together in my mind. My mother first broke silence.

"Poor, infatuated boy!" said she, the tears flowing down her cheeks, "what new calamity have you brought on yourself by your wild, inconstant disposition?" I told her I had enlisted, and was going that day to join my regiment—"Alas!" said she, "you have now finished it. Now you are lost to us and to yourself; but will you not come home, and see your father before you go?" I hesitated. "Perhaps," said she, "it will be the last time you may ever see him. Come, you had better go with me."

I consented, and we went home together. It was near four o'clock. My father generally came home at that hour to dinner. My mother met him as he came in, and explained matters to him. He strove to assume an air of calmness; but his countenance showed the emotions that were working in his mind. We sat down at the table to dinner; but no one seemed inclined to eat. My father cut some meat on his plate, but instantly pushed it from him. He rose from his seat, and walked about the floor with a rapid pace. He opened his waistcoat. He seemed suffocating. I could no longer endure to see the convulsive agony with which his whole frame was agitated. I sunk on my knees at his feet, and cried out, "Forgive me, O father—forgive me!"

He looked at me for a moment; then, bursting into tears, he said, "God forgive you! God forgive you! My poor unfortunate boy. Alas!" said he, "I had none but you. I had formed schemes for your advancement in life. I saw you had some talent, and was determined to spare no expense in making you fit to fill a respectable situation. I had figured to myself you going in and out with me, happy and contented—a credit to yourself and to your parents; but, alas! those hopes are now fled forever: for the first news I hear of you, may be, that your corpse is bleaching on the Continent—a prey to wolves and eagles." Then, as if correcting himself for drawing such a picture—"But your life is in the hands of God. Yet even now, are you not lost to me? May I not say that I am childless?—I give you my forgiveness freely, and also my blessing; and if you should survive, oh! may you never have a son that will cause you such agony as I feel at this moment. Farewell! my poor boy; I am afraid I may say, Farewell forever!"

With these words he rushed into an adjoining room, and threw himself on his knees, I suppose to pray for that son who had repaid all his kindness with ingratitude and disobedience.

My mother was wild with grief. It was the hour at which we were to march. I tore myself out of the house in a state of distraction, and joined the party, who were now on the road to Airdrie. My mind was in such a state of agitation, that I scarcely knew where I was going. I walked on before the party, as if some evil thing had been pursuing me, anxious, as it were, to run away from my own feelings.

I am scarcely conscious of what passed between that and Dunbar; it seems like a confused dream. But the parting scene with my father often recurred to my memory; and although it is now fifteen years since it took place, it remains in it as fresh as yesterday. The step I took at that time has been to me the source of constant and unavailing regret; for it not only destroyed my fair prospects in life, and fixed me in a situation that I disliked, but I believe it was the means of breaking the heart of a parent, whose only fault was that of being too indulgent. I felt sensible of his tenderness, and I am sure I loved him. But mine was a wayward fate. Hurried on by impulse, I generally acted contrary to the dictates of my own judgment—"My argument right, but my life in the wrong."

He has long gone to his eternal rest; but while he lived, he was a man—take him all in all—whose equal will be rarely found; for it could be truly said of him, that "even his failings leaned to virtue's side."

When our party arrived in Dunbar, where the regiment lay, after being finally approved, and the balance of my bounty paid, which was about four guineas, (after deducting necessaries,) I was conducted by the sergeant to the room where my berth was appointed. When he left me, I sat down on a form, melancholy enough. An old soldier sat down beside me; and, remarking that I looked dull, asked me where I came from, when I replied, "Glasgow."

I was immediately claimed as a townsman by some of the knowing ones, one of whom had the Irish brogue in perfection, and another the distinguishing dialect and accent of a cockney.

"You don't speak like natives of Glasgow," said I.

"Och! stop until you be as long from home as me," said Paddy, giving a wink to his comrades, "and you will forget both your mother-tongue and the mother that bore you."

"Ha' ye got yere boonty yet, laddie?" said an Aberdeen man.

"Yes," said I.

"Than you'll no want for frien's as lang as it lasts."

So I found; for every little attention was paid me that they could devise. One brushed my shoes, another my coat; and nothing could equal the many professions of goodwill and offers of service I received. There was a competition amongst them who should be my comrade, each supporting his offer by what service he would render me, such as cleaning my accoutrements, teaching me my exercise, &c. It appeared to me that I was set up at auction to be knocked down to the highest bidder. But I paid little attention to them. My mind was taken up, thinking of my folly, and ruminating on its consequences.

After holding a private consultation amongst themselves, one of them took me aside, and told me it was the usual custom for each recruit, when he joined the company, to give the men of the room he belonged to a "treat."

"How much?" said I, putting my hand in my pocket; for, in the passive state of mind I was then in, they would have found little difficulty in persuading me to give them all I had.

"A guinea," was the reply.

"Why didn't you ask two?" said an old fellow aside to the spokesman, when he saw me give the one so freely. He seemed vexed that he had not.

It was then proposed to go into the town, to purchase the liquor; and I, of course, must go along with them. Four or five accompanied me to town, and we met two or three more as if by accident. As we returned home, they lingered behind me a little, and appeared to be consulting about something. When they came up to me, one of them said, as I had been so free in treating them, they could not do less than treat me; and led the way into a public house for that purpose. One half-pint of whiskey was called in after another, all protesting that they would pay their share; but when the reckoning came to be paid, which amounted to seven or eight shillings, each asked his neighbour to lend him until he went up to the barracks. It turned out, however, that none of them had any money; and it ended in a proposal that I should pay the whole, and they would repay me on payday. This opened my eyes a little. I thought I could see a great deal of meanness and trick in their conduct; but I seemed to take no notice of it.

When night came, the room was cleared, and the forms ranged around. An old Highlander in the room had a pair of bagpipes, which with two fifes constituted our music, and when we were all assembled, the drinking commenced, handing it around from one to another. After a round or two, old Donald's pipes were called for, and the men commenced dancing with the women of the company. The stamping, hallooing, and snapping of fingers which ensued, intermingled with the droning sound of the bagpipes, was completely deafening. In the confusion some of the thirsty souls took the opportunity to help themselves out of their turn, which being observed, caused a dispute; and the liquor being expended, a join of a shilling a man was proposed to "carry on the glory." I was again applied to, and aided by this fresh supply, they kept up "the spree" until one o'clock in the morning. When some of them who had got drunk began to fight, the lights were knocked out, and pokers, tongs, and tin dishes were flying about in every direction. At last the affair ended by the officer of the guard sending some of them to the guard-house, and ordering the others to bed.

Next morning I was besieged, before six o'clock, by a band of the fellows who had got drunk the night before, begging me to treat them to a glass to "heal their head." I felt little inclined to drink at that hour, and expressed myself to that effect. They then asked me to lend them money to procure it, and they would repay me on payday. I gave them what they wanted, and I soon had the most of the men in the room at me on the same errand. In the course of the day I got my regimentals served out, and was sent to drill. After drill it was intimated to the recruits who had lately joined, that they ought to treat the drill-sergeant, by way of propitiating his favour. While we were talking, the sergeant who had conducted us to the regiment came up to bid us farewell.

"You are not going away tonight," said a recruit.

"I believe I will," said the sergeant, "unless you have anything to treat me to."

"You ought to give the sergeant a supper," said a man who had joined about a month before; "we gave our conducting-sergeant a supper."

It was therefore agreed that we could be no worse than the others, and he was accordingly invited along with our drill-sergeant. When night came, and we were going into town, it was moved that the sergeants of our companies ought to be invited also; of course it was insinuated that we would be no losers by so doing. When we were all met, between sergeants of companies and their friends, whom they had taken the liberty to invite, we were a goodly company.

The supper came in, and was done great justice to by the guests. Next came the drink, and when all hearts were warmed by the rum-punch, numerous were the protestations of friendship and promises of favour from the sergeants to the recruits, which were very soon forgotten. I was sitting next our conducting sergeant: beseemed very restless, and spoke often to a very loquacious sergeant who sat near him, who replied several times that it was too soon yet.

At last, however, when he found we were all pretty mellow, he rose and commenced his harangue with, "I say, lads, I dare say you are all very well pleased with Sergeant A?" This was assented to by all the recruits. "Well," said he, "I just wished to inform you that it is the usual custom for the recruits to give the sergeant who conducts them a present when they receive their bounty."

The acquiescence of all present showed how well the sergeant had chosen the time to make his proposition.

"What is the usual sum?" said one.

This question was put to our conducting sergeant: and after some hesitation, he very modestly replied, "five shillings each." The money was soon collected, and he pocketed it with great glee.

At a late hour we separated, and got home to our barrack-rooms without disturbance, having previously had leave from tattoo. Next day I was roused for drill at daylight; and after coming in, wishing to procure some breakfast, I was surprised to find my cash dwindled to a very few shillings. During the day, I was applied to by some of my comrades for the loan of more money; but I refused, alleging that I had little left. I could soon see that this information made a great impression on them; for the things which they had formerly been so officious in doing for me were now left to be done by myself; and amongst all those who had been so anxious to become my comrades, I could not find one now that would accept of me, and a new party of recruits joining I was soon altogether forgot.

Next day, having purchased some little things that I needed, I found my money expended; but I gave myself little uneasiness about it, as I had lent so much, and the following day was pay-day. When the men received their pay, I spoke to those who had borrowed the money from me, and said that I would be obliged to them for it; but how was I surprised when some of them swore I had never lent them a farthing, and threatened to beat me for presuming to say so! Others said they could not pay me at that time; and more of them laughed at my simplicity in expecting repayment of any money borrowed out of a bounty!

This is strange kind of justice, thought I; and leaving the room, I wandered down by the sea-side, thinking on the honest men I had got amongst. I heard the step of someone behind me, and turning round to see who it was, I perceived one of the recruits who had joined some time before me. His name was Dennis, he was an Irishman. I had remarked that he took no part with the others in their professions of kindness to me, and that on the night of the spree he had gone to bed without joining in it. When he came up to me, he said, " I have waited until now to speak to you, for I would not say a word while the bounty lasted, lest you might suspect that I was like the others; but now I have come to say that if you choose you can be my comrade, for mine left me before you came to the room, to go along with a recruit; and now that his bounty is finished, he wishes to come back again; but I hate such meanness, and would never associate with a fellow of his description; however, I think you and I will agree."

I was glad to accept his disinterested offer; and during all the time Dennis and I were comrades, I never had reason to repent it; for he was of a warm-hearted, generous disposition, and never flinched from me in distress. He had no education: he could neither read nor write; but he had a judgment which no sophistry could blind, and his acute Hibernian remarks often puzzled men who thought themselves better informed; besides this, he had a fund of honour that never would allow him to stoop to a mean action. One fault, indeed, he had in common with the generality of his countrymen, and that was, when he got liquor he was a thorough madman.

Dennis and I were now left to ourselves, to act as we pleased, and the "knowing boys" looked out for newer hands to fleece, some of them descending to very mean stratagems to get drink. I remember being in town with Dennis one evening, and having gone into a public-house to get a glass before we went home, one of those disgraceful animals came into the room where we were sitting, and after telling some rigmarole story, without being asked to drink, he lifted the glass from before us, and having said, "Here's your health," swallowed its contents. I was confounded at his impudence, and sat staring at him; but Dennis was up in an instant, and knocked him down, and, as he said himself, "kicked him for falling." The fellow never made any resistance, but gathered himself up, and crawled out of the room.

When he was gone—"By my faith!" said Dennis, "I think I gave the rascal the worth of his money—that is the only cure for a 'sponge.'"

"I wonder they have no shame," said I.

"Shame!" rejoined Dennis, "shame and they might be married, for any relationship between them!"

In a short time I began to recover my spirits, and when I had any spare time, I had recourse to my old favourites, which I obtained from a circulating library in the town. It is true I could not now dream so delectably of the life of a shepherd or a sailor; but I had the field of honour before me. To fight in defence of one's country, thought I—to follow the example of a Bruce or a Wallace, must be a glorious thing. Military fame seemed the only object worth living for. I already anticipated my acts of valour, charging the enemy, driving all before me, and coming back loaded with honour and a stand of French colours; receiving the praise of my commanding officer, and a commission. On I went in my career of arms, and it was impossible to stop short of being a general.

In these day-dreams of promotion and honour, I did not look particularly to the situation I was then in; or even very attentively at the intermediate ground I had to go over: but these were trifles in my estimation at that time. I must confess, however, that a damp was often thrown over these fine speculations by some harsh words from the drill-sergeant, or some overbearing conduct of my superiors. Or when I saw a poor fellow taken out, and receiving a flogging for being ten minutes late from tattoo, I could not help thinking the road to preferment rather rough. Be that as it may, I believe I had by this time caught a portion of military enthusiasm; and "death or glory" seemed very fine words, and often, when walking alone, have I ranted over the words which Goldsmith puts into the mouth of the Vicar of Wakefield, when his son leaves him to go into the army—"Go, my boy, and if you fall, though distant, exposed, and unwept by those who love you, the most precious tears are those with which heaven bedews the unburied head of a soldier."

The miserable retreat of our army to Corunna, and the account given of it by some of those who had returned, often lowered my too sanguine anticipations; but nothing could permanently keep down my ever active imagination. In this state of mind, I felt a relief from the melancholy I had previously sunk into; but still I was far from being contented; something was continually occurring which made me draw comparisons between my present way of living, and that which I had enjoyed at home. There were few of those with whom I could associate, that had an idea beyond the situation they were in:[1] those who had were afraid to show they possessed any more knowledge than their comrades, for fear of being laughed at by fellows who, in other circumstances, they would have despised. If a man ventured to speak in a style more refined than the herd around him, he was told that "Everyone did not read the dictionary like him;" or, "Dinna be gi'en us ony o your grammar words na." If a man, when accused by his superiors of something of which he was not guilty, ventured to speak in his own defence, he was called a *lawyer*, and desired to give no reply. If he said that he thought it was hard that he should be condemned without a hearing, the answer was, "Be silent, sir! *you have no right to think*; there are people paid for thinking for you—do what you are ordered, sir, right or wrong."

If he did not join with his neighbours in their ribald obscenity and nonsense, he was a Methodist—if he did not curse and swear, he was a Quaker—and if he did not drink the most of his pay, he was called a miser, a mean scrub, and the generality of his comrades would join in execrating him.

In such society it was a hard matter for a man of any superior information or intellect to keep his ground; for he had few to converse with on those subjects which were most congenial to his mind, and to try to inform his comrades was a vain, and by them considered a presumptuous attempt. Thus, many men of ability and information were, I may say, forced from the intellectual height which they had attained, down to the level of those with whom they were obliged to associate; and everything conspired to sink them to that point where they became best fitted for tractable beasts of burden.

---

1. This is not to be wondered at when we consider how the army was at that time recruited; it is very different now.

Blackguardism was fashionable, and even the youngest were led into scenes of low debauchery and drunkenness by men advanced in years. Many of the officers, who, at least, ought to have been men of superior talents and education, seemed to be little better, if we were allowed to judge from the abominable oaths and scurrility which they used to those under their command, and the vexatious and overbearing tyranny of their conduct, which was too often imitated by those beneath them.

It redounds much to the honour of those who superintend the discipline of the army at present, that the situation of the soldier has been much ameliorated since that period.

Let it not be thought, however, that there were not many exceptions to this general character which I have drawn, (some of whom I will have occasion to mention in this narrative,) who have shed a lustre around the military character that has often served to conceal its defects.

CHAPTER 6

Portugal

About the beginning of May, we got the route for Aberdeen. On the march I have nothing interesting to take notice of, unless the kindness which we experienced from the people where we were billeted on the road, particularly after we crossed the Firth of Forth.

We arrived in Aberdeen, after a march of ten days, where we had better barracks, and cheaper provisions than in Dunbar; but the barracks being too small, a number of our men were billeted in the town, and not being in the mess when pay-day came, it was a common thing for many of them to spend what they had to support them in drink; and some of them were so infatuated as to sell even their allowance of bread for the same purpose. They were then obliged (to use their own phraseology) to "Box Harry," until the next pay-day; and some of them carried this system to such a length, that it was found necessary to bring them into barracks, to prevent them from starving themselves.

If I may be allowed to draw a conclusion from what I have seen, the men's morals are no way improved by being lodged out of barracks; for, while here, the principal employment of many of them when off duty was drinking, and associating with common women; and I think, if anything tends to depreciate the character of the soldier in the eyes of his countrymen, in civil life, more than another, it is this habit of associating publicly with such characters. This total disregard of even the appearance of decency, conveys an idea to the mind that he must be the lowest of the low. But many of them seem to be proud of such company; and it is quite a common thing to meet them on the streets arm in arm.

This debasement of feeling and character, I imagine, arises from the system of discipline pursued by many commanding officers, which teaches the soldier to believe that he is a mere piece of machinery in the hands of his superiors, to be moved only as they please, without any accordance of his own reason or judgment, and that he has no merit in his own actions, independent of this moving power. Such a belief has naturally the effect of making a man so little in his own eyes that he feels he cannot sink lower, let him keep what company he may.

But let soldiers be taught that they have a character to uphold; give them to understand that they are made of the same materials as those who command them, capable of feeling sentiments of generosity and honour; let officers evince by their conduct that they believe that the men they command have feelings as well as themselves, (although it would be a hard task to make some of them think so;) let them be encouraged to improve their minds, and there will soon be a change for the better in the army—one honourable to all concerned.

The doctrine which teaches that men are most easily governed when ignorant, is, I believe, now nearly exploded; and I can say from my own experience, and also safely appeal to all unprejudiced individuals of the army, whether they have not found men having some intellectual cultivation the best soldiers.

We had been about three months in Aberdeen, when we received orders to hold ourselves in readiness to sail for Jersey; and four transports having arrived for us, we prepared to embark.

This was a busy scene. We had been on good terms with the townspeople, and many of them attended us to the pier. As we marched down the old women stood in rows, exclaiming—"Peer things! they are gaun awa to the slaughter."While the boys were ranked up, marching before our band, with as much importance as if they considered themselves heroes; and no doubt, the fine music, and the sight of the soldiers marching to it, gave them high ideas of a military life: and perhaps, was the incipient cause of their enlisting at a future period. Indeed, I must confess that when I heard the crowd cheering, and our music playing before us, I felt at least a foot higher, and strutted with as much dignity as if I had been a general. I almost felt proud at that moment that I was a soldier.

Once embarked, however, and fairly out to sea, my enthusiasm soon evaporated. Stowed like any other part of a cargo, with only eighteen inches allowed for each man to lie on, we had scarcely room to move. The most of the men became sea-sick, and it was almost impossible to be below without becoming so. The women particularly suffered much; being crammed in indiscriminately amongst the men, and no arrangement made for their comfort.

No incident of any consequence took place en this voyage, with the exception of a severe gale of wind, which forced us to run into Dungeness; but it soon abated, and proceeding on our voyage, we made the island of Jersey, and disembarked at St. Oban's harbour; from whence we marched through St. Helier's to the Russian barracks near Groville.

All kinds of liquor, tea, sugar, and fruit, were here un. commonly cheap; but bread was dear, and what we had served out as rations was quite black and soft., something in consistence like clay. Brandy was only a shilling a bottle; wine two shillings; cider three halfpence a quart; and tobacco fifteen pence a pound.

The jovial drinking fellows amongst us thought this another paradise—a heaven on earth; and many of them laid the foundation of complaints here which they never got rid of.

It was during the time we were here that the jubilee (on his Majesty's entering the fiftieth year of his reign) was celebrated. We were marched to the sands between St. Helier's and St. Oban's, where the whole of the military on the island were assembled. We were served out with eighteen rounds of blank cartridge per man, and the *feu-de-joie* was fired from right to left, and again taken up by the right, thus keeping up a constant fire until it was all expended. The artillery, with the various batteries, and shipping in the harbour, joined in the firing; and altogether formed an imposing scene.

When we arrived at our barracks, we got a day's pay in advance, and, with great injunctions not to get drunk and riotous, we were allowed to go and make ourselves merry until tattoo-beating. Dennis and I resolved to hold the occasion like the others, although he said he did not admire this way of "treating us to our own."

We went to one of the usual drinking-houses; but it was full, up to the door; volumes of tobacco-smoke issued from every opening; and the noise of swearing and singing was completely deafening.

We were obliged to go farther off to get a house to sit down in. At last we found a place of that description, and went in. After a glass or two, we became quite jovial; and Dennis insisted that our host and his wife should sit down along with us. He was a Frenchman, and spoke little English; but Dennis did not mind that, and there soon commenced a most barbarous jargon— Dennis laying off a long story, of which, I am sure, the poor man did not understand a syllable. Yet he went on, still saying at the end of every sentence, "You take me now?"—"You persave me now, don't you?" While our host, whose patience seemed pretty well taxed, would shrug up his shoulders with a smile, and looking at his wife, who seemed to understand what was said nearly as well as himself, he would give a nod and say:

"*Oui, monsieur*—yees, sare."

Dennis having got tired of talking, asked the landlord if he could sing. This completely puzzled the Frenchman. At last, after every method had been tried in vain to make him comprehend, Dennis said, "You do this," and opening his mouth, he howled out a line of an Irish song. The Frenchman, seemingly frightened with the noise that Dennis had made, started to his feet and—

"Me no *chanter.*"

"Och! the devil's in ye, for a liar, *parly-vu*. But no matter, I'll give you a song—a true Irish song, my jewel," and he commenced with *The Sprig of Shillelagh and Shamrock so Green*. He had got as far as "An Irishman all in his glory was there," quivering and spinning out the last line of the verse to a prodigious length, when a rap came to the door, and the voice of the sergeant of the picket, asking if there were any soldiers in the house, put an unpleasant end to his melody. Previous to this, however, Dennis had taken up a spade handle, to represent the shillelagh, and it was with difficulty that I prevented him from bringing it down on the sergeant's head.

We were then escorted to the guard-house, for being out after tattoo, which we found so full that we could scarcely get admittance. Dennis cried and sung by turns, until he fell fast asleep. I was so stupefied with the drink I had taken that 1 scarcely knew how I felt. Next morning, however, we were released along with all the others who had been confined the preceding evening.

We had been about three months in Jersey when the order came for our embarkation for Portugal; but only six women to every hundred men were allowed to accompany us. As there were, however, a great many more than that number, it was ordered that they should draw lots, to see who should remain. The women of the company to which I belonged were assembled in the pay-sergeant's room for that purpose. The men of the company had gathered round them to see the result, with various degrees of interest depicted in their countenances. The proportionate number of tickets were made with "to go" or "not to go" written on them. They were then placed in a hat, and the women were called by their seniority to draw their tickets. I looked round me before they began. It was an interesting scene. The sergeant stood in the middle with a hat in his hand, the women around him, with their hearts palpitating, and anxiety and suspense in every countenance. Here and there you would see the head of a married man pushed forward, from amongst the crowd, in the attitude of intense anxiety and attention.

The first woman called was the sergeant's wife—she drew

"not to go." It seemed to give little concern to anyone but herself and her husband. She was not very well liked in the company. The next was a corporal's wife—she drew "to go." This was received by all with nearly as much apathy as the first. She was little beloved either.

The next was an old hand, a most outrageous virago, who thought nothing of giving her husband a knock down when he offended her, and who used to make great disturbance about the fire in the cooking way. Everyone uttered their wishes audibly that she would lose; and her husband, if we could judge from his countenance, seemed to wish so too. She boldly plunged her hand into the hat, and drew out a ticket; and opening it, she held it up triumphantly, and displayed "to go."

"Hurrah!" said she, "old Meg will go yet, and live to scald more of you about the fireside."

A general murmur of disappointment ran through the whole.

"Hang the old wretch!" said some of them, "she has the devil's luck and her own."

The next in turn was the wife of a young man, who was much respected in the company for his steadiness and good behaviour. She was remarkable for her affection for her husband, and beloved by the whole company for her modest and obliging disposition. She advanced with a palpitating heart and trembling hand, to decide on (what was to her, I believe) her future happiness or misery. Everyone prayed for her success. Trembling between fear and hope she drew out one of the tickets, and attempted to open it; but her hand shook so that she could not do it. She handed it to one of the men to open—when he opened it, his countenance fell, and he hesitated to say what it was. She cried out to him, in a tone of agony, "Tell me, for God's sake, what it is."

"Not to go," said he, in a compassionate tone of voice.

"Oh, God, help me! O Sandy!" she exclaimed, and sunk lifeless in the arms of her husband, who had sprung forward to her assistance, and in whose face was now depicted every variety of wretchedness. The drawing was interrupted, and she was carried by her husband to his berth, where he hung over her in frantic agony. By the assistance of those around her, she was soon recovered from her swoon; but she awoke only to a sense of her misery. The first thing she did was to look round for her husband; when she perceived him she seized his hand, and held it, as if she was afraid that he was going to leave her. "O, Sandy, you'll no leave me and your poor babie, will you?"

The poor fellow looked in her face with a look of agony and despair.

The scene drew tears from every eye in the room, with the exception of the termagant whom I have already mentioned, who said, "What are ye a' makin' sic a wark about? let the babie get her greet out. I suppose she thinks there's naebody ever parted with their men but her, wi' her faintin', and her airs, and her wark."

"Oh, you're an oul hard-hearted devil," said Dennis, " an unfeeling oul hag, and the devil'll never get his due till he gets you;"—and he took her by the shoulders and pushed her out of the room. She would have turned on Dennis; but she had got a squeeze from him on a former occasion, and I dare say she did not like to run the risk of another.

The drawing was again commenced, and various were the expressions of feeling evinced by those concerned. The Irish women, in particular, were loud in their grief. It always appeared to me that the Irish either feel more acutely than the Scotch or English, or that they have less restraint on themselves in expressing it. The barrack, through the rest of that day, was one continued scene of lamentation.

I was particularly interested in the fate of Sandy and his wife. I wished to administer consolation; but what could I say? There was no comfort that I could give, unless leading her to hope that we would soon return.

"Oh, no," said she, "when we part here, I am sure that we'll never meet again in this world!"

We were to march the next morning early. The most of the single men were away drinking. I slept in the berth above Sandy and his wife. They never went to bed, but sat the whole night in their berth, with their only child between them, alternately embracing it and each other, and lamenting their cruel fortune. I never witnessed in my life such a heart-rending scene. The poor fellow tried to assume some firmness; but in vain: some feeling expression from her would throw him off his guard, and at last his grief became quite uncontrollable.

When the first bugle sounded, he got up and prepared his things. Here a new source of grief sprung up. In laying aside the articles which he intended to leave, and which they had used together, the idea seemed fixed in her mind, that they would never use them in that way again; and as she put them aside, she watered them with her tears. Her teapot, her cups, and everything that they had used in common—all had their apostrophe of sorrow. He tried to persuade her to remain in the barrack, as we had six miles to travel to the place of embarkation; but she said she would take the last minute in his company that she could.

The regiment fell in, and marched off, amid the wailing of those who, having two or three children, could not accompany us to the place of embarkation. Many of the men had got so much intoxicated that they were scarcely able to walk, and the commanding' officer was so displeased with their conduct, that in coming through St. Helier's he would not allow the band to play.

When we arrived at the place where we were to embark, a most distressing scene took place, in the men parting with their wives. Some of them, indeed, it did not appear to affect much; others had got themselves nearly tipsy; but the most of them seemed to feel acutely. When Sandy's wife came to take her last farewell, she lost all government of her grief. She clung to him with a despairing hold.

"Oh, dinna, dinna leave me!" she cried. The vessel was hauling out. One of the sergeants came to tell her that she would have to go ashore. "Oh, they'll never be so hardhearted as to part us!" said she; and running aft to the quarter-deck, where the commanding officer was standing, she sunk down on her knees, with her child in her arms. "Oh! will you no let me gang wi' my husband? Will you tear him frae his wife and his wean? He has nae frien's but us—nor we ony but him—and oh! will ye mak' us a' frien'less? See my wee babie pleadin' for us." The officer felt a painful struggle between his duty and his feelings: the tears came into his eyes. She eagerly caught at this as favourable to her cause, "Oh ay, I see you have a feeling heart—you'll let me gang wi' him. You have nae wife: but if you had, I am sure you wad think it unco hard to be torn frae her this way—and this wee darlin'."

"My good woman," said the officer, "I feel for you much; but my orders are peremptory, that no more than six women to each hundred men go with their husbands. You have had your chance as well as the other women; and although it is hard enough on you to be separated from your husband, yet there are many more in the same predicament; and it is totally out of my power to help it."

"Well, well," said she, rising from her knees, and straining her infant to her breast: "it's a' owre wi' us, my puir babie; this day leaves us friendless on the wide world."

"God will be your friend," said I, as I took the child from her until she would get into the boat. Sandy had stood like a person bewildered all this time, without saying a word.

"Farewell then, a last farewell then," said she to him. "Where's my babie?" I handed him to her—"Give him a last kiss, Sandy." He pressed the infant to his bosom in silent agony, "Now, a's owre; farewell, Sandy! we'll maybe meet in heaven:" and she stepped into the boat with a wild despairing look.

The vessel was now turning the pier, and she was almost out of our sight in an instant; but as we got the last glimpse of her, she uttered a shriek, the knell of a broken heart, which rings in my ears at this moment. Sandy rushed down below, and threw himself into one of the berths, in a state of feeling which defies description. Poor fellow, his wife's forebodings were too true! What became of her I have never been able to learn.

Nothing occurred worthy of remark on our voyage from Jersey to Lisbon. When we made the mouth of the Tagus, we got a Portuguese pilot on board. He had scarcely reached the gangway when he was surrounded by all the men on deck; for his appearance was grotesque in the extreme. He was about four feet and a half high, and had on a jacket and breeches of what would have puzzled a philosopher to tell the original; for patches of red, yellow, blue, &c., were mingled through the whole dress, without any regularity. A pair of red stockings, and an enormous cocked hat, completed his costume. His complexion was of the same hue as a well-smoked bacon ham; and the whole contour of his face bore a striking resemblance to the ape tribe.

"Blessings on your purty face, my honey," said Dennis, as he eyed him narrowly, "you have made your escape from some showman. May I never sin, if I don't think I have seen you tumbling on a rope at Donnybrook Fair."

Our hero passed on, taking no notice of the compliment Dennis had paid him, to take the helm from the seaman on duty; but the tar, giving him a contemptuous look, called out to the captain, "Will I give the helm to this here thing?"

"Certainly," said the captain, laughing. The sailor, however, did not seem sure about him; and, as he passed on to the forecastle, could not help throwing a doubtful look behind at his substitute. He proved to be a good pilot, however, and managed the vessel well.

We passed Fort St. Julian, and sailed up the Tagus as far as Belem, where our pilot gave the order to "let go de ank."

Next morning we disembarked and marched up to St. Domingo convent, part of which had been converted into barracks. In the course of the day Dennis and I got into the town. We promised ourselves much from the view we had had from the river the preceding evening; but were miserably disappointed when we got into the streets; for mountains of filth were collected in them, so that we could scarcely pass; and the smell of oil and garlic issuing from the shops was quite sickening. The most of the streets were very narrow.

The population seemed composed of monks and friars, for we

met them at every step either begging, or walking in procession with the sacrament (or host) to some sick person. On these occasions they were preceded by a bell, which warned the passengers of their approach; whenever it was heard, they were down on their knees in a moment, in the very middle of the mud, and continued praying and beating their breasts until it passed.

Poor Dennis was sadly puzzled the first time he met one of these parties: he was a Catholic, and of course could not avoid following the example of the *Christianos* around him; but he had a great aversion to kneeling in the dirty streets. The procession was fast advancing, and he had been two or three times half down on his knees and up again; at last, a lucky thought struck him—he snatched the hat out of the hand of a Portuguese who was kneeling before him, and deliberately placing it on the ground, kneeled down on it, and went through the ceremony with great gravity—thus saving both his conscience and his breeches. The fellow who owned the hat durst not move until the procession had passed; and then, without giving him time to speak, Dennis clapped the hat, dirty as it was, on the owner's head, and walked off.

The fruit market was opposite to the convent gate; and it certainly was to us a novel and a pleasing sight. The finest fruits, which at home were rare and high in price, we found here as plenty and as cheap as gooseberries. Pineapples, peaches, and grapes, of the largest size and most exquisite flavour, with oranges, lemons, and pomegranates, were arranged on the standings in the most tempting and tasteful manner. Dennis and I walked through amongst them with a strong desire of tasting them, yet fearful that our finances would not enable us to buy any. I ventured, however, to ask for the worth of a *vintin* (about three halfpence English) of oranges; after giving the woman the money, and pointing to the fruit, I held out my hand to receive them, but she beckoned me to give her my hat, and to our surprise, she nearly filled it.

The fragrant and delicious odour which perfumed the market-place, and the sight of the beautiful fruit and flowers, made it a much more attractive place of resort, than the dirty streets filled with the abominable stench which issued from their cook shops. My opinion of the interior of Lisbon was certainly very low; and I think, if a stranger wishes to see Lisbon, and leave it with any idea of its grandeur, he ought to contemplate it from the river, but never set his foot on shore, for he will then feel nothing but disgust.

CHAPTER 7

The French Surgeon

We remained only seven days in Lisbon: on the evening of the seventh we were turned out, marched down to Belem, and embarked by torchlight for Cadiz. I do not remember anything worthy of notice which took place on this voyage, only that it was tedious.

When we made the Bay of Cadiz, we found a large fleet of British vessels there before us. The French had possession of all the surrounding country, with the exception of the Isle of Leon and Cadiz; and these were closely besieged. When we first arrived, we were not sure on which side of the bay we might be required to land; but we were served out with flints and ammunition, and our commanding officer issued a circular to the men on board the different transports, ordering us to hold ourselves in readiness for immediate action, and exhorting us to remember the honour of our country and regiment.

That evening, our light company, with those of the other regiments, forming a light brigade, under the command of Major-General the Hon. Sir William Stewart, landed and marched to the outpost at the town of Isla. Next day, the remainder of the troops disembarked; and entering Cadiz, we occupied part of the bomb-proof barracks under the ramparts, where we remained with Lieutenant-General Graham, who was chief in command.

I could not say that our reception by the inhabitants, on landing, was very flattering. Here and there, amongst the crowd, you could hear a *"Viva Englese;"* but the greater number received us with a gloomy, suspicious silence. Setting aside other causes, it was really not to be wondered at, that the inhabitants should feel little attachment to the English, when we consider that they had suffered so severely by Nelson and the British fleet, about four years before, and that the shattered remains of some of their vessels were still lying in the bay.

Cadiz was, in my opinion, a much cleaner town than Lisbon, and in point of situation, more picturesque. From the ramparts on the Atlantic side of the town, the view was very fine: to the left, we could see the African shore, with its mountains stretching out until their outline was lost in the distance. Before you the prospect was unconfined, and the eye was lost in the wide world of waters, unless when it was arrested by a passing sail, or brought nearer the town by the noise of the breakers lashing the dark sides of the rocks, which ran out into the sea, and here and there showed their heads above water. On the side of the town next the bay, the Rota, Bay of Bulls, with the town of Port St. Mary's, Porto Real, Isla, Checuelina, and Cape Trafalgar, brought the eye round to where it set out.

When we had anything to wash, we were obliged to go outside the walls to some of the cisterns, a short distance from the town. It was here I first learned to wash my own clothes. I was awkward enough when I began, but practice soon made me expert at it.

In one of these washing excursions, I happened to pass a chapel; and seeing people engaged at some ceremony in it, my curiosity prompted me to enter. A corpse lay on a bier, with the face uncovered, and a bunch of flowers were placed in its hands, which were joined together in a praying attitude. The priest was performing the service of the dead over it; near him stood two little boys, with silver censers waving in their hands, filled with burning incense. The whole service seemed to me impressive enough. After it was finished, the corpse was removed to the outside of the chapel, and deposited in a hole in the wall resembling an oven; it was then covered with quick lime; the mouth of the hole shut up with a stone, which fitted it; and the people retired.

65

As yet, none of the troops had been brought into action, with the exception of the light companies, who had some slight skirmishing at the outposts. The French had attempted nothing of any consequence. They were very busy, however, prosecuting the siege—building batteries in every direction. There was one battery, called Fort M———. It lay on the French side, at the extremity of a point of land, stretching down from Porto Real into the bay, opposite to Puntallis. From this, had they manned it, they might have annoyed our shipping very much; and it was resolved that we should take possession of it.

Accordingly, one evening the three first men from each company of the regiment to which I belonged were turned out, in marching order, for that purpose. At the quay, we were joined by a detachment of artillery, and were conveyed across the bay in man-of-war boats. On our passage we were joined by a party of seamen and marines; who, with a captain-commandant, surgeon, two subalterns, one of whom acted as adjutant, a lieutenant of artillery, and a midshipman, made in all about one hundred and fifty men.

When we reached the fort, we used every precaution to avoid alarming the French if there had been any there; but it was quite unnecessary, for their picket had retired, without firing a shot. After placing a picket in front, we set to work, and got up three guns, which we had brought with us. This kept us busy enough until morning, when we got a better view of the isolated place we had taken possession of. The fort itself was about a hundred yards square; but it had been completely demolished on its sea face, by the seamen of our fleet when the French advanced to the siege, and the others were all more or less in ruins. The bomb-proofs were nearly all destroyed. In what remained there was not shelter for the half of our men; and by a rule of division, often practised in the army, that little was made less by the officers appropriating the half of it to themselves.

Day had not long dawned when the French gave us a salute from a small battery, in the village at Fort Lewis; but when we got our guns mounted, it was soon silenced. From that time we commenced with redoubled exertion to work at the battery—building up the parapets, and laying platforms for more guns. We were supplied with materials, *viz.* fascines, gabions, and sandbags, from Cadiz.

Here we were wrought like slaves, I may say, without intermission; for our worthy adjutant, who aimed at being a rigid disciplinarian, and was a great amateur in drill, was determined that no hard labour, or want of convenience for cleaning our things, should tempt him to deviate from a clean parade and formal guard-mounting every morning, even although we had been out all night under the rain on picket, or carrying sandbags and digging trenches up to the knees in mud. All the varied forms of duty known in a militia regiment, with which he was best acquainted, were by him deemed indispensable; and in a place where we had no convenience for keeping our things in order, not even shelter for them, this exactness was certainly, to say the least of it, unnecessarily teasing. We were also obliged to stand sentry on different parts of the battery, full dressed, where there was no earthly use for us, unless for show; and I could perceive no reason the commandant and he had for their conduct, unless that, feeling the novelty of their situation—in command of a fort—they wished to ape, with their handful of men, all the importance of leaders of an army.

We were driven from guard to working—working to picket—picket to working again, in a gin-horse round of the most intolerable fatigue; which we never could have borne for any length of time, exposed as we often were to sun and rain, in a climate like that of Cadiz. But, even with all this, we had the mortification to find our best endeavours repaid with the most supercilious haughtiness, and the worst of usage. We were allowed little time to sleep; and that little often interrupted.

But let it not be imagined that our officers participated in all this fatigue: they knew how to take care of themselves; and they could sit and drink wine in their bombproof at night, as comfortably as in a mess-room at home. And it was a common amusement of the commandant, when he got warmed with it, to order the drum to beat to arms in the middle of the night— when the poor wretches, who had perhaps just lost sense of their fatigue in sweet oblivion, would be roused up, and obliged to go to their several posts on the ramparts; and when permitted to go below to our berths, we would scarcely be lain down, when we were again roused to commence working. This was the usual routine the most of the time we were here.

It may be well to remark, however, (for the benefit of those officers who may wish to follow the example,) that the commandant had a most ingenious method of assembling his men quickly: he used to stand, with his fist clenched, at the top of the ladder leading from the bombproof, ready to knock down the last man that came up; and as someone must necessarily be last, he of course was sure of the blow; and as he was a strong muscular man, it used to tell (as we military men term it) on the poor fellow's head.

One man, I remember, who had suffered in this way, remonstrated, and threatened to complain to his colonel; but the answer was a second "knock-down," and an order to confine him between two guns in an angle of the battery, where he was exposed to the inclemency of the weather for many days and nights without covering; and when his health was impaired by this usage, he was still kept in the fort, although it was the usual practice to send the sick to the general hospital in Cadiz. He was not allowed to leave the place until we all left it; and then it is probable, if he had ventured to complain, he might have been flogged in addition to all he had suffered, for presuming to say anything against the Hero of M———.

We had now got up six guns and two mortars on the fort, which was all we could mount to have any effect. We were supported by a Spanish man-of-war and six or eight gun-boats; and with them, we used to bombard the small village at Fort Lewis, and annoy the working parties coming down from Porto Real to build batteries. We often made great havoc amongst them, with spherical case-shot. One day in particular, I remember, we brought down an officer who was riding on a white horse at the head of his party, and we saw them carry him off in a litter from the place where he fell.

About this time a severe gale came on, by which a great number of vessels were stranded on the French side of the bay; most of them were abandoned by their crews, who got safe over to Cadiz; but one transport, containing the flank companies and staff of a battalion of the fourth regiment, ran ashore near Port St. Mary's, and they were all taken prisoners. They had their colours with them, and I heard afterwards that they had put them under the coppers and burned them, rather than let them fall into the hands of the enemy. Many of these vessels were richly laden; and as they were sure ultimately to fall into the hands of the enemy, being also considered fair prizes when they ran ashore on an enemy's coast, we procured a couple of boats, and succeeded in securing part of the cargo of those nearest us, which was principally silk, with some pipes of wine and salt provision.

The stranded vessels, that lay along the shore, were often visited by straggling parties of the French, who used to carry off heavy burdens of the cargo. This stimulated some of our men to follow their example; but there was great risk in the adventure. They could only go at night, and run all hazard of their absence being discovered: that, however, might be averted by the sergeants, who, of course, shared in the booty; but the marsh which they had to cross was very dangerous, the road uncertain, and they might have been taken by the enemy's pickets; but notwithstanding these obstacles, there were many, who, either out of a spirit of adventure, or a love of gain, despised them all, and were well repaid for their trouble by the valuable articles which they found.

Our party often fell in with the French stragglers, who were there on the same errand; but they were quite friendly, and when any wine or spirits were got in the vessels, they used to sit down and drink together, as sociably as if they had been comrades for years. What every man got was his own, and there was seldom any dissension.

One night, I happened to be of the party. We had made our burdens, parted with our French friends, and left the vessel on our way to the fort. The party of the French had left it also. We had not proceeded far, when we missed one of our comrades; and fearing that some accident had befallen him, we returned, and near the vessel saw him struggling with someone. We hastened up to him; but before we reached the spot, the person with whom he was engaged fell to the ground, with a groan. At that moment, we saw our comrade stoop, and tear something from him.

"What is the matter?" said one of our party.

"Come away," said he, " and I'll tell you as we go along;" and he passed us on his way to the fort.

We were anxious to see who his antagonist was; and on raising him up, we found that he was one of the French party, who had been with us in the vessel. He had been stabbed in the left side with a Spanish knife, which still remained in the wound. One of the party withdrew it. The blood flowed out of the wound with great force. The poor Frenchman gave a deep groan—a convulsive quiver—and expired.

"This is a horrid, cold-blooded murder," said I. "Where is S——?"

At this moment we heard thenoise of footsteps approaching, and thinking it might be the comrades of the Frenchman who had been barbarously assassinated, we left the place precipitately, our minds filled with horror at the savage deed.

On our way to the fort, we overtook S——; but none of us spoke to him. He, however, strove to extenuate his conduct, by saying that he observed the Frenchman find a purse in a chest that he had broken open, and seeing him linger behind his party, for the purpose of secreting it about his person, he went up to him, and asked a share of it. The man refusing this, a scuffle ensued, and he stabbed him in his own defence, the Frenchman having attempted to stab him. We knew this to be false; for the Frenchman had no weapon in his hand, or near him; and we had no doubt, from what we knew of S——'s character, that he had perpetrated the murder for the sake of the money, which was gold doubloons. He offered to share it with us; but not one of us would touch it; and from that time forward he was shunned and detested by all who knew of the murder. He never prospered after. I even thought that his countenance acquired a demon-like expression, that rendered it repulsive; and we had not been long in Portugal, when he went to the rear and died in great misery. After that we never returned to the vessels.

The Spaniards had a number of hulks moored in the bay which Lord Nelson made for them, on board of which they kept their French prisoners, who, we understood, were very ill used, nearly starved, and huddled together in such a way that disease was the consequence. Many of them died daily. They were kept until sunset, and then thrown overboard, and allowed to float about in the bay. Every tide threw some of them ashore, and the beach was continually studded here and there with them. When our men discovered any of them, they scraped a hole in the sand, and buried them; but they were totally unheeded by the Spaniards, unless when they practised some barbarity on them—such as dashing large stones on their heads, or cutting and mutilating them in such a way that the very soul would sicken at the idea.

I was one night on picket, and along with the sergeant reconnoitring the ground in front of the fort, as the French pickets were in the habit of coming close down on us when it was dark. We saw something white moving amongst the weeds near the shore, to the left of the battery, and we went down in that direction to see what it was; but in an instant we lost sight of it. When we came to the place where we first saw it, we found the body of a man extended on the ground. This was not an uncommon appearance; but as we had seen something moving when we were first attracted to the spot, I was induced to feel the body, to ascertain whether it was dead, and to my surprise, I found him warm, and assisted by the sergeant, raised him up. It struck us that he had only fainted, and we rubbed him for some time with our hands. He at last began to recover, and his first action, when he came to himself, was to fall down on his knees at our feet, and cry *"Misericordia."*[1] We did not understand what he said; but we asked him, in English, how he had come there. Whenever he heard us speak, he sprung to his feet, and seizing our hands, he cried *"Vous etes Anglois—Grace a bon Dieu!"*[2]

We threw a great-coat over him, and took him into the fort, where, placing him before a fire, and giving him some bread and wine, the poor fellow soon recovered. When it was discovered that he had no clothes on, one man took off his shirt and put it on him, another gave him a pair of trousers, and he was soon comfortably clothed. He poured out his thanks in French, but he saw we did not understand the language. He tried the Spanish with like success. He attempted a mixture of both with as little effect; but when he pressed his hand on his heart, and the big drop gathered in his eye, he found by the sympathizing tear which it excited, that no words were necessary to express the universal language of gratitude.

When he was perfectly recovered, we reported the affair to the commandant, and the artillery officer speaking the French language, he was questioned by him. In reply, he said he was a surgeon in the French service; that he had been taken prisoner and confined on board one of the prison-ships; that that night he determined to make his escape, or perish in the attempt; and having lowered himself down from one of the gun-ports, quite naked, he had swam a distance of two miles; but was so exhausted when he reached the shore, that he sank down insensible at the time we had first seen him; when he recovered, his first idea was that he had fallen into the hands of the Spaniards, who, he well knew, would have butchered him without mercy; but when he found by our language that we were English, he was overjoyed. He had saved nothing but a miniature of a female, which hung round his neck, and which he seemed to prize very much; for when he recovered, the first thing he did was to feel if it were still there, and raise it to his lips and kiss it.

---

1. Mercy.
2. Thank God you are English.

He was kept until next day in the fort, when he was sent over to Cadiz. He seemed distracted at the idea of going there, lest he should be delivered over to the Spaniards; and although he was assured to the contrary, still he seemed to feel uneasy.

It was not many days, however, after that when he was sent back, with orders that he should be escorted to our outposts at night, and left to join his countrymen. When night came, he took leave of the men in the fort with a kind of regret. I again happened to be of the party who escorted him. After leaving our picket, the sergeant and I conducted him up the pathway leading direct from the fort, until we suspected that we were near the French picket, and there we told him that we would be obliged to leave him. He pressed our hands in silence: his heart was too full to speak; but we could easily guess what were his emotions. Joy at the idea of again rejoining his own countrymen, with a feeling at parting with those to whom he considered he owed his life, were contending in his mind.

The night was dark, and we soon lost sight of him; but we lay down on the ground, and listened with anxious suspense, afraid that the French outpost sentry might fire upon him before he had time to explain, and he might thus lose his life on the very threshold of freedom; but we did not hear the sentinel challenge him, nor did we hear any shot fired. We had therefore every reason to believe he reached his countrymen in safety.

During the time we were here, an attack was meditated on the French positions, and a number of troops were landed on the fort for that purpose. A strong party of seamen was also landed at Fort Catalina, who succeeded in storming it, and spiking the guns; but in consequence of some signals being thrown up by adherents of the French in Cadiz, they were alarmed, and the troops were obliged to return without effecting what had been originally intended.

CHAPTER 8

The Siege

We had now been in the fort about two months; and from the time that we had silenced the small battery that had opened on us, when we first gained possession of the place, the French had not molested us, although they occasionally fired shots at the boats passing up and down the bay. We were well aware, however, that this was! only a deceitful calm before a storm; for they had been busy all this time building batteries both in front and to our right in the village I have already mentioned, although they were hidden from our view by the houses.

At last, when everything was prepared, they commenced their operations one night by blowing up the houses which had hitherto masked the batteries. I was out on picket at the time; and we perceived them moving round a large fire which they had kindled. We suspected that they designed to attack us, and our suspicions were soon verified; for in a short time after, they gave a salute of grape-shot, which ploughed the earth on every side of us; but this was only a prelude. A volley of red-hot shot, at the Spanish man-of-war, succeeded, which set her on fire, and obliged her to slip her cable, and drop down the bay. A volley or two more of the same kind scattered our gun-boats; and we were then left to bear the brunt of the battle alone. Now it began in earnest. Five or six batteries, mounting in all about twenty guns, and eight or ten mortars, opened their tremendous mouths, vomiting forth death and destruction. The picket was called in.

There was a number of spare fascines piled up on the sea face of the battery, amongst which, for want of room in the bomb-proof, we formed huts. In one of these I lodged. They had been set on fire by a shell that fell amongst them; and when I entered the fort, the Spanish labourers were busy throwing them into the sea. I ran to try to save my knapsack, with the little treasure which I had gained; but it was too late—hut and all had been tossed over. There was no help for it: I did not know how soon I might be thrown over also. I was called to my gun, and had no more time to think on the subject. They were now plying us so fast with shell, that I saw six or eight in the air over us at once.

Death now began to stalk about in the most dreadful form. The large shot were certain messengers where they struck. The first man killed was a sailor who belonged to the *Temeraire*, seventy-four. The whole of his face was carried away. It was a horrid-looking wound. He was at the same gun with me.

"Ah! what will we do with him?" said I to a seaman next me.

"Let him lie there," was the reply. "We have no time to look after dead men now."

At that time I thought it a hardened expression; but this was my first engagement. Not so with the tar. He had been well used to them.

The French soon acquired a fatal precision with their shot, sending them in through our embrasures, killing and wounding men every volley. I was on the left of the gun, at the front wheel. We were running her up after loading. I had stooped to take a fresh purchase, a cannon-ball whistled in through the embrasure, carried the forage-cap off my head, and struck the man behind me on the breast, and he fell to rise no more.

The commandant was now moving from place to place, giving orders and exposing himself to every danger. No one could doubt that he was brave: had it been bravery, softened and blended with the finer feelings of humanity, he would have been a true hero; but —— our artillery officer behaved like a gentleman, as he had always done; and our subaltern in a tolerable medium: the midshipman in the style of a brave, rough, and ready seaman.

But, alas, how had the mighty fallen!—our brave adjutant, whose blustering voice, and bullying important manner, had been always so remarkable, was now as quiet as a lamb.. Seated in an angle of the battery, sheltered from the shot, no penitent on the *cutty stool* ever exhibited so rueful a countenance.

The carnage now became dreadful; the ramparts were strewed with the dead and wounded; and blood, brains, and mangled limbs, lay scattered in every direction: but our men's spirits and enthusiasm seemed to rise with the danger. The artillery officer stood on the platform, and when he reported any of our shot taking effect, a cheer followed, and " At it again, my heroes!" was the exclamation from every mouth. When any of our comrades fell, it excited no visible feeling but revenge. "Now for a retaliating shot!" was the word; every nerve was strained to lay the gun with precision; and if it took effect, it was considered that full justice was done to their memory.

We had a traversing gun in the angle of the battery which had done great execution. The artillery sergeant commanded her; and they were plying her with great vigour. In the course of the day, however, as the man was returning the sponge after a shot, and the cartridge in the hand of another, ready to reload, a thirty-two pound shot from the French entered her muzzle, she rebounded, and struck the sergeant with her breech on the breast, and knocked him over insensible. The shot had entered so far that she was rendered useless, and abandoned.

The action was kept up the whole of that day, during which we lost the best and bravest of our men. Our guns had been well directed at first; but, towards evening, the most of the artillerymen who had commanded them were either killed or wounded; and the direction of them was then taken by men who knew little about it. The consequence was that much ammunition was used to little purpose. The artillery soldier at the gun next to me was killed, and two men, equally ambitious for what they considered the post of honour, quarrelled about it. From high words it came to blows; but the dispute was soon settled; for a shell, falling between them, burst, and quieted them forever.

I could scarcely define my feelings during the action; but so far from feeling fear, when it first commenced, and the silent gloom of the night was broken by the rapid flash, and the reverberating thunder of the cannon, I felt a sensation something resembling delight; but it was of an awful kind—enthusiasm and sublimity, mixed with a sense of danger—something like what I have felt in a violent thunder-storm.

The firing, on both sides, had been kept up without intermission from two o'clock in the morning; but as it now became dark, it was partially suspended. I then, for the first time ventured to go below to the bomb-proof. The scene there was dismal—the wounded filled the whole place, and the doctor had not got through with the dressing of them. In this he was materially assisted from the commencement of the action by a female, Mrs. Reston. It is matter of surprise to many, that the courage she displayed, and the services she rendered on that occasion, should have been entirely overlooked by those who had the power of rewarding her, or that her claims on the country were not more warmly seconded by the officer who commanded in the fort.

Here let me pause in my narrative to pay a tribute of respect to the memory of assistant-surgeon Bennet, who was with us during that trying period. To a fair knowledge of his profession, he added one of the kindest dispositions I ever knew anyone possessed of; he was absolutely without one drop of gall in his composition; so much so, indeed, that some of the officers endeavoured to make him a butt for their raillery, but his native wit defeated their purpose, and turned against them their own weapons. Those who have been under his care will remember him with grateful feelings. But his career was brief; shortly after our arrival in Portugal, he caught infection from some of the sick whom he was attending, and died.

During the day I had little time to reflect on anything—all was noise and bustle; but now that I had time to look round, and saw the ramparts covered with the pale and disfigured corpses of those who, a few hours before, were rioting in the fullness of health and strength, and others writhing in agony, under the severe wounds they had received, I could not deny that I felt my heart sink within me, and sensations of a melancholy and solemn nature took place of those which had before excited my mind.

When daylight came in next morning, the firing again commenced as warmly as the preceding day; and the precision the French had attained with their shot was very remarkable. We had a flag-staff of the usual size, on which was hoisted the Spanish colours. They had cut it across with a cannon-ball, it was repaired, and again replaced; but it was not five minutes up, when another shot brought it down again. This occurring four or five times successively, gave great offence to the sailors, who attributed all that we had suffered to fighting under the Spanish flag, and swore that if the Union-Jack were up in its place, the French would not bring it down so easily.

"There's that bloody Spanish flag down again," said one of the tars.

"Look ye, Jack! I have got our boat's ensign here—let me go, and I'll soon run it up."

He went, and assisted in repairing the flag-staff; but instead of again bending the Spanish flag to the halliards, he put the English in place of it. A general huzza greeted its appearance.

"Now, hang it! we'll beat the French dogs," said the seamen; but the cheering attracted the notice of the commandant, and he ordered it to be hauled down again. Never was an order so reluctantly obeyed. In a few minutes, a shot cut through the flag-staff.

"There it goes down again—Oh, botheration!" was the surly reply. "Let it lie there:" and there it lay, for no one would meddle with it.

"Better to fight without a flag at all, than under such a bloody treacherous flag as that," said an old sailor. "I never could bear it, unless when I saw it flying at the masthead of an enemy."

By this time three of our guns were rendered unfit for service, and they had made great impression on our parapet, with a breach in the end of the bomb-proof. A corporal of our grenadier company had gone below to get some refreshment, and was raising a tin with some wine in it to his mouth, when a shot entered the breach, and striking some small arms that were placed against the wall, shivered them to pieces. One of the splinters entered his head, and he fell dead on the spot. The rest wounded several of the men beside him.

A shell fell about the same time at the magazine door. A blanket was the only partition between it and the powder. We were sure all was over—that it was impossible but that the magazine would be blown up. We stood in awful suspense for the few seconds between its fall and bursting—it burst—and already we imagined ourselves in the air; but fortunately, it did not communicate with the powder. There were two artillerymen in the magazine at the time, whose feelings could not be very enviable.

In the course of the morning, General Stewart came over from Cadiz to inspect the state of the fort, when it was found that it could not stand out much longer. A reinforcement of men from different regiments was sent over to assist us, in case of the enemy attempting to storm us in our disabled state, but we received little assistance from them.

One of our sergeants, who, from his complexion, was called the "Black Prince," had installed himself commissary; and on the pretence of preventing the men from getting drunk, he seated himself beside the cask, which contained our ration wine, and fulfilled his duty so faithfully that he would not even give the men their allowance, but gave it away very liberally to any of the strangers who could "tip him the blarney;" and among hands "he did not forget himself." He got rather tipsy at last; and the men getting clamorous for their just allowance, to settle the dispute, he staved the cask, and spilt the wine about the place.

Let it be observed, however, that I do not blame the action, had his motive been to prevent the men getting intoxicated, (the best proof of which, would have been keeping sober himself;) but as the contrary was obviously the case, it could only be attributed to caprice, for he withheld the ration allowed from many of the men, while he distributed to others what they chose to ask.

The affair was scarcely worth mentioning, only that it will serve to show on what an uncertain basis a soldier's fame rests; for he was extolled to the skies, and subsequently got a situation in the commissariat department for that action; while others, who had distinguished themselves by their valour and intrepid exertions, were passed by unnoticed.

It being found that we could not keep the place, boats were sent to convey us to Cadiz. Mines had been previously laid, and a major of engineers came over to superintend the operations for blowing up the fort; but he had not taken many paces on the battery, when he was struck by a cannon-shot, and fell a lifeless corpse.

It is remarkable to observe the covetousness of some men, even in the midst of danger. When he fell, the epaulettes were torn off his shoulders, and the gold watch was taken out of his pocket. The watch was afterwards recovered, but not, I believe, until the chain and seals were disposed of.

The men were now busy gathering what things they had together, and moving down to the boats. Some of them had already sailed. I had now time to reflect on the almost naked situation in which I was left, for I had thrown off my great coat at the commencement of the action, and someone had taken it away. I ran down to the bomb-proof, to try if I could find anything to put on, but I met an engineer officer at the end of the passage, with his sword drawn, who had been inspecting the train laid to the mine. He asked me if I wished to be blown up, and ordered me off instantly.

On coming up the ramparts I found that all the men had left the fort, with the exception of three or four, and the commandant. He was watching the motions of a strong party of French, who were evidently coming down to take the place. Our ammunition was expended, but he ordered all the loose powder, grape, and ball cartridge to be collected, and having stuffed three guns (all we had left fit for service) to the muzzle with them, we watched the enemy until within about two hundred yards of the battery, when they were fired into the very middle of their column, and laid the half of them prostrate on the earth; the rest wheeled to the right about and left us to embark at leisure.

A number of the men who had been killed were lying on the ramparts. Some of them of the same regiment to which I belonged. We resolved on giving them some sort of burial, as the last kind office we could perform. We gathered them into a temporary hut, which had been built of mud, and, throwing it down over them, "Sleep there, brave comrades!" said we: "far distant, and ignorant of your fate, is the wife or mother who would have composed your mangled limbs." Hurried and rude was their burial, and a heartfelt sigh all their requiem, but it was more valuable than the ostentatious trappings of affected woe.

We then hurried down to the boats; they were all gone but one, and after entering, I learned from my comrades that two men of the party who had come to reinforce us had got themselves so beastly drunk that they could not stir, and had been left behind.

We were not a great distance from the fort when it blew up, but only partially. The French were still firing, and one of the shells falling into a boat, which preceded us, burst and killed three men, besides wounding others. We were taken by the boats on board of the *Invincible* seventy-four, where we were very kindly treated; from that we were conveyed to Cadiz.

The regiment I belonged to had removed to Isla Camp, but we were marched up to our old barracks in the bombproof, and a motley-looking group we were. Half-naked, and blackened with the smoke of the gunpowder, we looked more like chimney-sweepers than soldiers. We were received very coolly by the Spaniards. They did not seem to feel any commiseration for us on account of what we had suffered. I imagined their looks expressed vexation rather at any of us escaping alive.

When we reached the barrack, exhausted with fatigue and want of sleep, I threw myself on the stone floor. My mind was a chaos. The events of the preceding thirty hours were all jumbled together in my brain. Previous to that I had a good assortment of necessaries, with a hundred and fifty dollars, and some pieces of silk. I was now left with a pair of canvas trousers, my shirt, shoes, and forage cap; but it was the fortune of war, and I soon forgot it all in a profound sleep. I do not know how long I slept; but when I awoke all my comrades had left the bomb-proof, away drinking, with the exception of one or two, who had been left as poor as myself.

I had received a wound in the leg from a splinter of a shell during the action. At the time I paid little attention to it, but it had now become so inflamed and swelled that I could scarcely move it. My former excitement of mind, with the fatigue I had endured, had produced a proportionate debility, and my feelings were no way enviable. Nothing could be more lonely, desolate, and heartless, than the state in which I felt myself the remaining part of that day.

CHAPTER 9

Recovering from Wounds

The day following, we marched to join the regiment at Isla Camp. Our comrades turned out to receive us, and our hearts thrilled with exultation at the encomiums passed on our bravery. The poor fellows flew with alacrity to procure wine to treat us; amongst the rest, my comrade Dennis was not backward. He and I had been separated when I went to the fort, and he was now overjoyed to see me. He seized my hand in the warmth of his heart, and shook it so long, and squeezed it so heartily, that I was ready to cry out with the pain.

"Man alive, Joseph!" exclaimed he, "is it yourself that's in it? troth, I thought I'd never see you more, for, when I saw the shot and shell flying about ye like hailstones, I said to myself, 'Poor comrade! it's all over with you;' but, thank God, here you are safe and sound."

"Scarcely," said I.

"What's the matter, my dear fellow, are you wounded?"

"Slightly, but that is not the worst of it, I have all my kit on my back."

"Och, if that's all, never fear, my boy—you'll never want while Dennis has a shirt in his knapsack, or a cross in his pocket."

And his were not empty professions; my heart glows with grateful feeling to this moment at the remembrance of his disinterested kindness. In my chequered journey through life I met few friends of his description.

After supplying me with things to change myself, he procured a canteen of wine; and being joined by more of our comrades, who were willing to show their goodwill, and who had come equally well provided, we sat down in the tent, and I soon forgot all that I had suffered.

When the wine warmed my head, I entered into a detail of our proceedings during the time we were in the fort, and with a feeling of pride and exultation—"fought all the battle o'er again." My comrades, ranged around, greedily devoured the relation; and their exclamations and remarks served to heighten my enthusiasm. I can smile now at the warmth of my feeling, and the high ideas I had then of a warrior's fame. Yet, I must say, that there is a feeling connected with military enterprise, which will scarcely fail to carry all before it, particularly in men of any imagination. Military glory, or fame, calmly considered, certainly appears a mere bauble, an *ignis fatuus*: but show me the man, of any soul, who could take this view of it in the midst of battle: there the imagination soars unconfined beyond every trammel, and gets into the region of sublimity and enthusiasm.

Next day we were called out. The regiment formed square, and the remains of our party was marched into it. We were then addressed by our commanding officer in terms of the highest eulogy, and held out to the regiment as a pattern. The sergeant who had distinguished himself by staving the wine cask, was particularly addressed, and told that he would not be lost sight of. We were then dismissed; but with the exception of this sergeant, I do not remember any of us who were thought of after the speech. For my own part, I know that I found difficulty enough in getting the sum of two pounds eight shillings, in lieu of all that I had lost! The commandant, however, was soon raised to the rank of major, and not long after to that of lieutenant-colonel.

The regiments of the brigade in camp were busily employed at this time working at the batteries, which were building on the island; for which they received ninepence per day, in addition to their pay. They had also extra rations, such as coffee and sugar for breakfast, and a pint of porter daily; but the labour was very hard, and the exposure to the sun brought on sickness amongst them.

Still we had little reason to complain, for we were under the command of a general who did not think it below him to look into the men's rights and interests, and anticipate their wants. It was not an uncommon thing, in a very wet morning, to find him up at our camp, ordering an extra ration of rum to be served out to the brigade. There were also double tents provided for us; as, in consequence of the heavy rains, the single ones were found insufficient; and on every occasion he paid the most indefatigable attention to our comfort. In him was found a rare combination of the rigid disciplinarian and the soldier's friend. He discharged his own duty faithfully and well; and he expected everyone under him to do the same, and would admit of no excuse for the non-performance of it from either officer or soldier. To those who served under his command, in that place, it will be unnecessary to say that the officer to whom I allude, is Lieutenant-General the Hon. Sir William Stewart. His name will be associated in their minds with the character of a gallant and able officer, and a steady friend to the soldier.

We generally turned out for the working party at five o'clock in the morning; and our breakfast, which was coffee with bread, was always ready at that hour. I remember, the first time we had it, each man came forward with his mess-tin for his allowance, which was measured out by the cook. We had a Highland man in the company, who had enlisted raw from his native hills, and who, I believe, had never seen anything of the kind before. When he came for his allowance of the coffee, which was now nearly done, the cook was skimming it off the top very carefully, to avoid stirring up the grounds. Donald, who thought this a scheme to keep all the good part to himself, exclaimed, "Tarn your plod! will you'll no gie some o' the sik as well as the sin?"

"Oh, certainly," said the cook, (who was a bit of a wag,) and stirring the grounds well up, he gave him a double proportion.

Donald came in, chuckling with satisfaction at having detected the knavery of the cook, saying, "If she'll socht to sheat a Highlandman, she'll be far mistook;" and seeing the rest of his comrades breaking bread in their coffees, he did the same: by this time the eye of everyone in the tent was on him, scarcely able to refrain from laughing. Donald began to sup it with his spoon; but after taking two or three spoonfuls, grinding the coffee-grounds between his teeth, and making wry faces, he threw the tin, contents and all, out of the tent door, exclaiming, "Tarn their coffee! you might as weel chow heather, and drink pogwater as that teevil's stuff. Gi'e Donal a cog o' brochan before ony o' your tea or coffees either."

The French had once or twice made a powerful attack on our pickets, but were repulsed with loss; and the skirmishing at our outposts, and firing from the batteries, were now carried on almost without intermission. We expected them to make an attack on us with their whole force; and scarcely a night passed without being turned out, in consequence of movements making on their side; notice of which was communicated to the troops by different coloured rockets, thrown up at our outposts.

At this time we had a strong force of British here. Besides artillery and engineers, we had a battalion of guards, and nine or ten regiments of the line. There was also a strong fleet of British vessels in the bay: at one time we had three first-rate men-of-war, namely, the *Caledonia*, *Hibernia*, and *Ville de Paris*, besides seventy-four gun ships, frigates, and a great number of smaller vessels and gunboats. Batteries were built on every commanding situation: one of which (St. Fernando) we used to call the Friar's battery, having been built in part by these gentry, and certainly among the best deeds they had done in that part of the country. It was on a very commanding situation, extending completely across the Isthmus at its narrowest part, with a wide trench, which could be filled with water from the sea on either side.

At this time the wound on my leg, to which I had paid little attention, became so ill that I was obliged to go into the hospital; and I, in a great measure, lost sight of what was going on amongst the troops. I had now nothing to relieve the monotony of an hospital life, unless a visit from Dennis now and then, when he could gain time from working or duty; and one visit from a sergeant (a townsman), who joined the regiment at that time, and had brought a letter from my parents. He had been long on the recruiting service, and was considered a first-rate hand at it. After some inquiries respecting my friends and native place, I happened to remark how successful he had been in getting recruits, and expressed my surprise that he should have been so much more so than others who had been on the same service. He replied, " No wonder at it—no wonder at all. I knew Glasgow well. It was my own place—knew the minds of the young fellows better than they did themselves—for I had been a weaver myself, and a lazy one too. I knew how I used to feel. In winter it was too cold, and in summer too warm to work. When it was good trade, I could not resist the temptation of drinking and going idle two or three days in the week; and when it was bad, I had no time to work for trying to find out the cause, and setting the government to rights. The truth is, you could scarcely ever catch a weaver contented. They are always complaining. Therefore, you would never have much trouble enticing them to enlist, if you knew how to go about it; or much in going after them, for whenever they got lazy, they came up and lounged about the Cross. You could not manage them, however, the same as a bumpkin. They were too knowing for that. The best way was to make up to the individual you had in your eye, and after bidding him the time of the day, ask him what sort of web he had in. You might be sure it was a bad one; for when a weaver turns lazy his web is always bad: ask him how a clever, handsome-looking fellow like him could waste his time hanging seesaw between heaven and earth, in a damp unwholesome shop, no better than one of the dripping vaults in St. Mungo's church, when he could breathe the pure air of heaven, and have little or nothing to do, if he enlisted for a soldier—that the weaving was going to ruin, and he had better get into some berth, or he might soon be starved. This was, generally, enough for a weaver; but the ploughboys had to be hooked in a different way. When you got into conversation with them, tell how many recruits had been made sergeants, when they enlisted—how many were now officers. If you saw an officer pass while you were speaking, no matter whether you knew him or not, tell him that he was only a recruit a year ago; but now he's so proud he won't speak to you; but you hope he won't be so when he gets a commission. If this won't do, don't give up chase—keep to him—tell him that in the place where your gallant honourable regiment is lying, everything may be had almost for nothing—that the pigs and fowls are lying in the streets ready roasted, with knives and forks in them, for the soldiers to eat, whenever they please. As you find him have stomach, strengthen the dose, and he must be overcome at last. But you must then proceed quickly to work, before his high notions evaporate. You must keep him drinking—don't let him go to the door, without one of your party with him, until he is passed the doctor and attested."

"But," said I, "you would not find everyone so easily duped."

"To be sure," said he, "some of your sentimental chaps might despise all this, but they were the easiest caught after all. You had only to get into heroics, and spout a great deal about glory, honour, laurels, drums, trumpets, applauding worlds, deathless fame, immortality, and all that, and you had him as safe as a mouse in a trap.

"But, if all these methods failed, and the fellow remained obstinately determined against parting with liberty, the next resource was to pretend you had been joking with him—that you had no wish to enlist any man against his will—that you had advised many a one not to enlist. Ask him in to take a friendly glass, ply him briskly, send one of your party out to put on plain clothes; let another of your men bring him in as a young man wishing to enlist, set him down next to the man you have in your eye. After allowing them some conversation, put the question to them, if they were talking about enlisting. 'Yes, I'll enlist,' would be the reply of your man, 'if this young man will go also.' Perhaps he might; but if not, your last resource was to get him drunk, and then slip a shilling in his pocket, get him home to your billet, and next morning swear he enlisted, bring all your party to prove it, get him persuaded to pass the doctor, as it will save the *smart* should he be rejected. Should he pass, you must try every means in your power to get him to drink, blow him up with a fine story, get him inveigled to the magistrate in some shape or other, and get him attested; but by no means let him out of your hands."

"At this rate," said I, "men are taken into the service by as unfair means as they are pressed on board a man-of-war. Were you not afraid of complaints being made to your officers; and did the magistrates not scruple to attest men who were drunk?"

"Not at all, man," was the reply. "It was war times. As for the magistrates, we knew who to go to on these occasions. You know it was all for the good of the service."

"But had you no honour or conscience of your own?" said I.

"Honour or conscience!" said he, laughing. "Pretty words in the mouth of a private soldier. You must do your duty, you know. A good soldier does what he is ordered, right or wrong."

"But I am afraid," said I, "that you did more than you were ordered."

"Perhaps we were not ordered to do all that we did; but we were blackguarded if we didn't get men, and that was the same thing; and what's the use of a man if he can't take a hint?"[1]

"You must have made a good deal of money in this way."

"Money!" said he, "No, no. Did you ever hear of men making money on the recruiting service? They must have come from the north if they did. No, our money didn't do much good—it all went in raking and drinking. 'It melted awa' like snaw aff a dyke,' as the old woman at home would say, and we left Glasgow with bad kilts, and worse constitutions."

"Well," said I, "you may be glad you have left it, for more reasons than one, and I hope you will never return to it."

The conversation was dropped, and he soon left me; but I could not help thinking how many poor fellows were thus inveigled into a profession they did not like, and rendered miserable the remainder of their lives.

---

1. I do not know whether the sergeant exaggerated or not; but, in justice to the service, I must remark that such stratagems are neither authorized nor resorted to at present.

While here I was near losing my life in a very simple manner. There was a garden behind the hospital, which had formerly been a gentleman's house, kept by a Spanish gardener, who raised vegetables for the Isla market. In it there was a cistern, from which the water ran when required to water the garden; and this was supplied by a contrivance very unlike anything I have seen in Britain, although common enough on the Continent. It was raised from a deep well, by means of pitchers attached to the circumference of a large wheel, which, revolving by the power of a horse and gin, were successively filled and emptied into the cistern. To this cistern the men who were able brought their things to wash; but the gardener, who either thought that the soap used spoiled his vegetables, or from sheer crossness, tried every means in his power to prevent them.

One day, while here dabbling my linen, he came to the cistern in a rage, and seizing my shirts he threw them into a dung-hill close by. This act was far from pleasing me, and I applied my fist to his ear, in a very unceremonious manner. This he returned, as is the usual custom with Spaniards, by drawing his knife, and making a thrust at me. I saw there was no safety unless in closing with him, to get it out of his hand; but as I got in upon him, he made a lunge at me, and drove it through my coat and shirt, grazing my ribs. I seized the hand which held it with both of mine, and tripped up his heels. We both came to the ground. He was now foaming at the mouth. I could not disengage his hand; and it would have been a doubtful thing who would have prevailed had not some of my comrades come into the garden at that moment. They freed his hand from the knife, which they withdrew and threw it into the cistern. They then left me to manage the Spaniard as I best could, which I found no difficulty in doing, as he could not use his fists with much effect. He, however, managed to bite me several times, before I had done with him.

I was obliged to be extremely cautious after this, as long as I was in the hospital; for I often saw him lurking about, eyeing me like a tiger watching his prey, and, no doubt, if he could have got an opportunity, he would have despatched me.

We had little opportunity of knowing much about the Spaniards here; but what we did know gave us no great idea of them, particularly the lower class. They seemed to be a jealous-minded, vindictive, and cowardly race, grossly ignorant and superstitious. Their soldiers are complete scarecrows, (I speak of them as I found them in every part of Spain,) badly clothed, ill paid, and worse officered. There could not be imagined a more barbarous-looking grotesque assemblage of men in the world than a Spanish regular regiment. No two men are dressed alike—one wants shoes, another a coat, another has a slip of blanket, with a hole cut in the middle, and his head thrust through it, a lapel hanging before and another behind. It is a rare thing to find one of them with his accoutrements complete; and their arms are kept in such order, that if brought into action, the half of them would be useless. On the march they have no regularity—just like a flock of sheep; and such chattering amongst them, that you would take it for the confusion of tongues at Babel!

They rarely ever succeeded at anything unless guerrilla fighting, and then only when they could take their victims by surprise, or when they were double or triple the number of their enemy.

There are certainly many brave and noble souls amongst them, whose hearts beat high in the cause of liberty, and who have evinced it by their gallant enthusiasm; but unfortunately they are but a small number, in comparison to the millions who are sunk in slavish ignorance and superstition.

CHAPTER 10

Looting

We had been about seven months in Cadiz, when the regiment to which I belonged was again embarked; and after a passage of eleven days landed at Lisbon. We remained there two or three days, making preparation for our advance; and were then conveyed in boats up the Tagus to Villa Franca, on our way to join the grand army under the command of Lord Wellington. From Villa Franca we marched to the convent of Alcantara, situated in a bleak moor; it had been wholly deserted by the monks, and the interior of it completely destroyed.

From that we moved to Rio Mayor, where we were for the first time quartered on the inhabitants; they seemed comparatively settled and happy to those of other places, where the troops had more frequently passed. The site of this village was beautiful—the river, from which it took its name, glided past it in silent majesty, skirted with rows of large trees; between which could be seen the sloping fields of maize, interspersed with vineyards, where the bunches of large purple-coloured grapes were peeping forth, half hid by the green foliage with which they were surrounded, tempting, as it were, the passenger to try how deliciously they tasted; and some of our men could not resist the temptation, although they were forbidden fruit.

There was something about this village so calm and serene, combined with the simple scenery around, which forcibly brought back to my imagination the Sabbath in a country village on the banks of the Clyde. I almost considered myself at home; and when I left it a day after, I felt grieved, as if leaving a place with which I had been long acquainted.

After halting one day here, we proceeded on the main road as far as Cavallos. Here we received information, from men going to the rear sick, that our army was retreating, after having fought an action at Busaco. This intelligence was soon confirmed by cars coming in with the wounded—those who had suffered slightly were walking, while others, whose wounds were more severe, were either sitting or lying on the cars, which from their construction were ill calculated for conveying sick and wounded men. They wore about five feet long, and two and a half broad; but instead of being boarded at the sides, there were stakes placed in holes about eighteen inches apart; the wheels were about two feet in diameter, rather octagonal than round; and as they were not girt with iron, it was quite a common thing to have a piece broken out of the circumference, and of course every time the wheel turned, the whole car was violently shaken. This was drawn by a pair of oxen, yoked by the head. A peasant, with a long stick and a sharp nail in the end of it, walked before them, and every now and then run his goad into their shoulders to hasten their pace. This generally produced an awkward zigzag trot for a few yards, when the jolting occasioned by the inequality of the wheels, caused the most excruciating torture to the poor fellows who were in them, and forced them to groan with agony. In this manner, exposed to the inclemency of the weather, and going at the rate of two miles an hour, they had to travel to Lisbon, a distance of forty or fifty miles, before they reached an hospital. The wounded continued to pass during the remaining part of the day, and throughout the whole night.

The continual creaking of their wheels was intolerable. I know of nothing in this country I can liken it to, unless the grating of an iron door on rusty hinges, but it was still worse than that. The Portuguese never put any grease on their wheels; for they think the noise of them frightens away the devil. The consequence is, that the axle tree often takes fire with the friction, and burns completely through. I never after could bear the noise of those cars. The hideous grating sound was always associated in my mind with the pallid faces and piercing groans of the wounded whom we that day saw passing.

Next morning we got orders to march across the country to Alcobaco, where we were to join the third division of the army, commanded by General Picton. This was a beautiful little village, with a very large convent in it, occupied by Bernadine monks—one of the richest orders in Portugal. It was built by Alphonso the First, to fulfil a vow made by him after the taking of Santarem from the Moors, and for its support he endowed it with all the land within view of its walls, which was not a little, for the prospect was extensive.

When we entered the village, we found it empty of inhabitants; for they had fled with precipitation when they heard that our army was retreating, leaving everything behind them, but what money or jewels they could carry about their persons. We were quartered in one of the passages of the convent. The monks had all left it, with the exception of a few who remained to superintend the removal of some of their precious articles.

I forget how many hundred monks there were cells for in the convent; but an idea of its size may be formed, when it is known that a whole division of the army, consisting of not less than live thousand men were lodged in the galleries alone, without filling them. Attached to it was a spacious chapel, the whole inside of which was decorated in the most superb style; the walls covered with valuable paintings, and in it a magnificent organ.

In the convent was the library, which contained a selection of many thousand volumes, with philosophical apparatus.

Contiguous to the church belonging to the convent there was a Gothic mausoleum of hewn stone, in the midst of which were two magnificent sepulchres of white marble, containing the remains of Don Pedro the First of Portugal, and of Dona Ignes de Castro—a description of whose tragic death forms a beautiful episode in the third book of the *Luciad*.

The kitchen of the holy fathers, which was on the sunk floor, presented a scene of plenty, which was not very favourable to the opinion of their severe abstinence. It was about a hundred feet long; the fire-place, which was raised on cast-iron pillars in the centre of the apartment, was thirty feet long, by twelve wide; a stream of water ran through the kitchen, which was occasionally overflown to cleanse the floor, and also supplied the tanks in which they kept live fish. Certainly, if they lived as well every day as they seemed to do while we were there, they could not boast much of fasting; for, in their larders and kitchen, there was a profusion of every delicacy which could be thought of. Their cellar contained upwards of seven hundred pipes of the choicest wines, and in the gardens belonging to the convent were the rarest and finest fruits, besides vegetables and plants of every description.

To judge from what we saw, they ought to have been the happiest fellows imaginable. Good eating and drinking, fine grounds to walk in, and plenty of books! What could they wish for more? It is likely, however, that their usual mode of living was not so luxurious as we were inclined to think, from what we saw of their kitchen; but I suppose they considered it better to use what they could of their dainties, than leave them to the French; and, to tell the truth, the poor monks did not seem to have any great appetite while we were there: for any of our men who entered the kitchen were liberally supplied with anything that was cooked.

Previous to the regiment being dismissed, the colonel cautioned us against taking anything which had been left by the inhabitants. Before the division came in, I believe this order was punctually obeyed, and our men walked peaceably up and down the streets, the same as they would have done in a village at home; but when the other regiments, composing the division, arrived, the scene was soon changed; for they scarcely took time to take off their knapsacks, before they commenced breaking up the doors, and plundering everything they could lay their hands on.

Some of our men, considering, I suppose, that they might as well have a share of the spoil as the others, joined in the throng;

but they had a lesson to learn which some of them paid for rather dearly. They were not aware that there was a provost-marshal[1] attached to each division.

And while they were busy he came upon them with his guard: the old campaigners made good their retreat, but our innocent boys, (as the Irish regiments in the division called them,) not being acquainted with his person or power, kept their ground, and were so warmly received, that they did not forget either him or his kindness while in the division.

An inspection was made next day of the division, to ascertain whether they had any plunder in their knapsacks, and anything found more than the regulated complement of necessaries was taken from them. The town fell into the hands of the French the following day, and it may be thought that it would have been better to allow us to take the things left than that they should fall into the hands of the enemy; but nothing is more subversive of discipline in an army than the habit of plundering, exclusive of the men, through covetousness, burdening themselves in such a way that they cannot march. Whether the means used to prevent it were the best and most efficient, I do not pretend to say; but there can be no doubt as to the necessity of preventing it as much as possible.

In the course of this day, the monks who had been left departed in chaises, and took not a few boxes of doubloons with them. The greater part of the pipes of wine in the cellars were staved, to prevent them falling into the hands of the enemy. We left the convent that afternoon, and having marched as far as Torres Vedras, encamped outside of the town.

When I say encamped, I do not mean that we pitched tents, for the army were not supplied with tents, until the campaign in 1813-14. At this time, the blue canopy of heaven was all our covering, the earth our bed, and a single blanket our bed-clothes.

A newly ploughed field, on the face of a hill, was our portion.

---

1. The provost-marshal is invested with power to inflict summary punishment on all soldiers whom he may find plundering, or straggling from their regiment.

We got out our blankets, and lay down, expecting to get a comfortable nap, although the weather was rather cold; but towards morning, it began to rain so heavily that we were soon wet to the skin. Some, who had a little wisdom in their heads, got up, and packed up their blankets; but others lay still, until they were literally floated with water and mud, which came rolling in streams down the ridges, in such a way that they could scarcely be distinguished from the soil around. They were then obliged to get up, and squeeze their blankets in that wet and dirty state into their knapsacks.

The rain got heavier the longer it continued, and we stood huddled together, shivering with cold and wet. At last an order came for us to march into Torres Vedras; but such a march I never saw, even in the worst of times afterwards. We were novices in the business, and not yet weather-proof. Had it not been that the town was so near, we would have occupied three or four miles of a line of road, we were so straggled. The ground was of a clayey nature, and with the rain that fell it had become like birdlime. Our feet stuck fast at every step, and our shoes were actually torn off, and many of them were left lying in the clay. Some were walking barefoot; others in their stockings, without shoes; and more had one shoe on, and another carrying in their hand. We were a set of drenched and miserable looking creatures, and the officers were in as bad a plight as ourselves.

At last we reached the town and got into houses; but the village was too small, and we were crowded in such a way that we had scarcely room to sit down. In the course of the day, however, arrangements were made; and some of the regiments sent to other villages, so that we were better accommodated.

During the time we were in the Peninsula, the troops suffered much from exposure to rain; and nothing renders a solders so uncomfortable as having wet clothes about him; or, I believe, hurts his health more, when first exposed to it. I have often wondered that no means were taken to prevent this. Many of the officers had oilcloth cloaks that completely covered them. Some such thing for the men would have been neither expensive nor heavy to carry, and would have been the means of saving many lives. Much more attention ought also to be paid to the quality of the shoes served out to the army, for they in general are of the very worst kind, and it was no uncommon thing for our store shoes to be in tatters before we had worn them a week.

After a stay of a few days here, we removed to Cadaciera in the same line of position, which extended from the Tagus to the sea. We had not long taken up our quarters in the village, where our whole brigade was, when a peasant entered it, driving a flock of sheep before him. In a moment, a race was made amongst them by some of the soldiers. Others, stimulated by their example, followed; and in a few minutes officers and men were seen promiscuously scrambling for the mutton. Dennis joined in the throng, and had seized one of them, at the same moment that an officer of the Irish regiment in the brigade made a grasp at it.

"Give me that sheep, sir," said the officer in an authoritative tone.

"Arrah, be aisy, honey!" said Dennis. "Kill a Hessian for yourself, if you plase."[2]

The officer relinquished his claim, and pursued another. The poor Portuguese shepherd stood like a statue, not knowing well what to do. At last, when he found himself relieved from all his charge, he went away lamenting and muttering curses on the *"ladrones Englese"*[3] to make his complaint to the general.

Soon after, a wine store was found out, and as plundering was the order of the day, the contents of it were soon lessened. This depredation was discovered by the men becoming intoxicated. The most severe investigation and search took place, and those with whom any of the stolen property was found were confined, tried by court-martial, and flogged; but they were not the most guilty who suffered.

---

2. I asked Dennis what the expression meant. He said that during the rebellion, a number of Hessian soldiers had been in Ireland, and a "United Man," having shot one of them, was busy plundering him, when one of his comrades asked share of the booty. "Kill a Hessian for yourself, my gay fellow," was the reply.
3. English robbers.

While we remained in this position, we were obliged to be under arms two hours before daylight, and remain until clear day; and for a few days after, these two hours were pretty well occupied by flogging. Terror seems to be the only engine of rule in the army; but I am fully persuaded in my own mind that if a more rational method were taken, the character of the soldier in quarters would be as exemplary as in the field. I cannot adduce any reasonable excuse for this wanton breach of honesty; for we were regularly supplied with rations at the time; but I imagine that most of the men were led into it by the example set by others, without taking time to think about the impropriety of the action. The soldier could scarcely think that there was any harm in the deed which an officer joined in. This was rather rare, however: but many of them had no objection to participate in what was stolen, which to me appeared equally blameable.

When settled in a place for any time, the brigade assembled on Sundays for divine service. We were always in full marching order on these occasions: and not uncommonly had a field day after it. If a person were to judge from the hitching of knapsacks, and wry faces that were making during this ceremony, he would have thought the soldiers would rather have dispensed with it; but I dare say, the anticipation of the drill that was to follow, prevented them from feeling much benefit from their devotions.

The first Sunday after the outrage already related, when the chaplain left his station, General Picton took his place.

This was the first time he had addressed us. I felt anxious to examine the features of a man who had been so much the public talk on account of his reputed cruelty at Trinidad. I could not deny that I felt a prejudice against him, and his countenance did not do it away: for it had a stern and gloomy expression, which, added to a very dark complexion, made it no way prepossessing; but when he opened his mouth, and began to pour forth a torrent of abuse on us for our conduct, and his dark eye flashed with indignation, as he recapitulated our errors, "hope withering fled, and mercy sighed farewell." He wound up the particular part of his speech addressed to us with, "You are a, disgrace to your moral country, Scotland."' That had more weight than all his speech. It sunk deep in our hearts. To separate a Scotchman from his country—to tell him he is unworthy of it—is next to taking away his life.

But General Picton was not the character which we, by prejudice, were led to think him. Convinced of the baneful effects of allowing his men to plunder, he set his face sternly against it, but in other respects he was indiligent; and although no man could blame with more severity when occasion required, he was no niggard of his praise when it was deserved. Nothing could surpass his calm intrepidity and bravery in danger; and his presence in battle had the effect of a talisman, so much had his skill and valour gained the confidence of the men under his command.

CHAPTER 11

Sabugal

From Torres Vedras, we removed to Alcoentre, a small village some miles in rear of Rio Mayor; and we were kept pretty busy while in it, strengthening our position, making batteries, breastworks, abattis, &c.

The general of the brigade was quartered in the same village; and as he had, or seemed to have, a great antipathy to everything Scottish, our regiment of course was included, and he found means to annoy us a good deal. Perhaps, he believed, with many people in England that the Scots run wild about their native hills, eating raw oats like horses, with nothing but a kilt to cover their nakedness, and that they had no right to receive any other treatment, when they entered the army, than what is usually given to any wild animal when caged. "Rousing up with a long pole" seemed to be his hobby. When exercising in the field, our regiment could do nothing right. When our guard turned out to salute him, they were either too late, or they did not present arms properly; and he would order the sergeant to drill them for an hour; while he stood by and gave vent to the harsh epithets which he was in the habit of using on those occasions: "Scottish savages—stupid—barbarous," &c.

I have often been led to think that he studied expletives on purpose. He pretended that he could not understand a word that any of us said—that we spoke Gaelic; and his aide-de-camp was called to interpret, although he had no right to understand what was said better than himself, for I believe he was also an Englishman.

As a sample—he once took a fancy to the wooden cases which the Portuguese use instead of stirrup-irons, and ordered his Scottish servant to get a pair for him; for although he disliked the Scots, he employed them as his servants. The man procured them; but they were not fellows.

"Well, sir," said the general, "have you got those things?"

"Yes, sir, but they are no marrows."

"Marrows! marrows! what's that? what's that?" and calling his aide-de-camp, he asked him what "the Scottish savage" said.

"He means, sir, that they are not fellows."

"Poh! poh! you surely do not pretend to understand what is no language."

"That is his meaning in his own language, sir."

"Nonsense, sir, you are as bad as he; go and read your dictionary."

He was very strict in duty affairs, particularly in details, which perhaps another general would not have troubled his head about. He was very fond of surprising the sentinels at the outposts, by taking circuitous routes, and keeping under cover of the bushes. On one occasion, however, he met with his match, if the story reported was true: but as I only had it from report, I will not pledge myself for its truth.

One of the men on picket was planted as outpost sentry on the road leading to Rio Mayor.

"Now, George," said the corporal to him, as he was leaving him, "mind that the general is out in front, keep a good lookout, or he may surprise you, and you know the consequence. Be sure you challenge in time."

"Leave that to me," said Geordie.

A short time after (it was dusk when he was posted), he heard someone coming up the road very cautiously, as if wishing to avoid observation. At last, when about to turn the road, the individual, who was on horseback, clapped spurs to his horse, apparently for the purpose of passing him before he could challenge. There was no time to lose, and many a poor fellow might have been so confused at being taken unawares, that he would have neglected to challenge before the person was on him. Not so with Geordie. The moment he saw him quicken his pace, he challenged. The challenge was either not heard or purposely unheeded. Another challenge was given; the general continued his gallop without answering.

"You'll no tak me in that way, my gentleman," said Geordie; and as he gave the third and last challenge, he came to the present, and made a bullet whiz past the general's ear. The horse was drawn in immediately.

"What! do you mean to shoot your general, you rascal?"

"I dinna ken wha folk are in the dark; but whether you're a general or no, my orders are to fire at ony body that attempts to pass me without answering when I challenge. It's the general's orders; and I ken what I would get if I didna obey them."

"Well, sir, I am your general; and I wish to pass into the town."

"I'm no sure about ye—ye may be some French spy for ony thing I ken; and ye maun just stay whar ye are till the sergeant o' the picket comes; he'll no be lang now, for the report o' my piece would alarm them."

At that moment the picket arrived, and the general was allowed to proceed; but from that time, he did not trouble the outpost sentries so much.

Some time before we left these quarters to advance, an attack was made by the French, under General Junot, on our advanced posts; and we were ordered under arms to defend our position, in the event of their pushing forward. During that day, and the succeeding night, the baggage of the troops in front, along with the inhabitants of the surrounding country, filled the road leading through our village. It was a melancholy sight to see the poor natives, carrying their children, and any little thing which they were able to bring with them, moving along the road, after having left their homes and property—travelling they knew not whither, desolate and friendless. In a few days they might be reduced to beg, or perhaps (what was not uncommon in Portugal) die of hunger. Alas! thought I, what misery war causes! I hope I will never see my own country in such a state.

The French were beaten back, and our troops resumed their former station; but few of the inhabitants returned.

Not long after this, we were reviewed, along with a part of the first division, by Lord Wellington. From the place where we were assembled, we could see Santarem, General Massena's headquarters. Next day (the 6th of March) the whole army was ordered to advance, as the French had retreated in three divisions, by separate routes during the night.

This opened the campaign of 1811. From Alcoentre we marched to Rio Mayor (our former quarters when we were on our way to join the army); but it was sadly altered—the inhabitants had mostly all left it; the houses were in ruins; and it wore a desolate appearance. Next day we crossed to Alcaneyde. From thence we proceeded to Porto do Mos.

When we entered the latter place there was a large convent fronting us, which, as well as many of the houses, had been set on fire by the French. I never before witnessed such destruction. The finest furniture had been broken up for firewood; the very floors torn up, beds cut in pieces, with their contents thrown about, intermixed with kitchen utensils, broken mirrors, china, &c. &c, all in one heterogeneous mass of ruin, and not an inhabitant to be seen.

We had scarcely taken up our quarters, until I was called out for duty, and placed on the commissary guard. The mules with the stores had arrived, and the storekeeper looking for a place to put them in, when we joined him. At last he pitched on a chapel for the purpose. There was a large fire in the middle of the floor, on which was heaped broken pieces of the altar, wooden images, frames of pictures; even the ornamented woodwork of the organ was broken up for the purpose.

In searching for the clearest place to set down the bags of biscuit, we found a door leading to some place apart from the chapel. As it was quite dark, I caught up a burning piece of wood to inspect the place—but what was my horror, when I entered and found the half consumed skeletons of human beings on every side; some lying, others kneeling, and more of them standing upright against the walls. The floor was covered with ashes, in many places still red. I stood fixed to the spot—the burning stick dropped from my hand. I informed some of my comrades of what we had seen, and we re-entered. Such an appalling sight was never witnessed. Of those who had sunk on the floor, nothing remained but the bones; while the others, who were in a kneeling or standing posture, were only partially consumed; and the agonized expression of their scorched and blackened features was awful beyond description.

On going to the upper end of the apartment, I perceived a bag lying on the floor with something in it. I was almost afraid to open it, lest some new object of horror should present itself. I was not mistaken in my apprehension; for when the bag was examined, it was found to contain the dead body of an infant, which had been strangled; the cord used for that purpose still remained about its little neck.

Next morning we continued our march to Leria, and on entering it found it burned. We were quartered in a convent outside the town, which was partially consumed, where we remained the succeeding day.

On the top of a hill, to the left of the town, was a sort of redoubt. I went with Dennis to take a view of the place, and going up to where some of our soldiers were standing, we found three children lying, two already dead, but the other was still breathing. There were pieces of biscuit lying beside them, which our soldiers had brought—but it was too late. They had evidently perished from hunger; one of them had expired with the bit in his mouth. This was part of the horrors of war; but only a part. The wanton cruelty of the French soldiers, on this retreat, defies description.

From Leria we advanced towards Pombal, in front of which the French army had concentrated their force and made a stand; but they retired during the night, and took up a strong position at the end of a defile between Pombal and Redinha, with their right on a wood, and their left occupying the high ground above the river of Redinha, the town being in their rear. In this position our division attacked their left, the light division their right, and the fourth their centre; the rest of our army being in reserve.

Their right was soon dislodged from their position in the wood, and retreated across a narrow bridge over the Redinha, followed by our light troops; but as the fords and bridge were commanded by their cannon, some time was lost before a sufficient number of troops could be passed over, to make a new disposition to attack the heights on which they had taken post. A portion of the division crossed the river by swimming, headed by Major Lloyd: but the columns moved on towards the bridge. As we were advancing, a cannon-shot from the enemy struck our column, killed a sergeant, and wounded two or three men; besides tearing our armourer's knapsack open, and scattering its contents about in every direction—the poor fellow was so frightened that he grew sick, went to the rear, and soon after died.

Our troops having passed the river, we soon drove them from their position back upon the main body, and next day their whole army was strongly posted at Condeixa. Our division was ordered to march through the mountains on their left towards the only road open for their retreat, which had the effect of dislodging them from their strong position; here our part of the duty was very fatiguing, for the hills were so steep that we had to scramble up the one side on our hands and feet, and slide down in the same manner on the other.

The French had retreated in such haste from their position at Condeixa that they left the communication with Coimbra unguarded, and our army communicated with Colonel Trant and the Portuguese militia, who were in possession of it.

They were now obliged to abandon all the positions which they had successively taken in the mountains, and their rear guard was thrown back on the main body at Miranda de Corvo, from which they immediately retreated, destroying part of their ammunition and baggage. At this place we passed many dead bodies of French and Portuguese, lying on the road; and one part of it was covered with asses, which the French had hamstrung before they left them. It was pitiable enough to see the poor creatures in this state; yet there was something ludicrous in the position that the animals had taken, when thus cruelly lamed; they were sitting in a group upon their hinder end, staring in each other's faces, seemingly in deep consultation on some important subject, and looking as grave and dull as many an assembly of their biped brethren at home.

The enemy now took up a new position on the river Ceira, leaving a division at a small village as an advanced guard, which was attacked by the third and light division, and after some hard fighting their army retired across the Ceira during the night, destroying the bridge. The enemy suffered severely here, for besides their killed and wounded, numbers were drowned in crossing the river.

Having taken up another position, from which they were driven by our division, with the first, and light, they concentrated their whole army on the Sierra Moito, from which they retired on the eighteenth, and our army occupied the ground they had left. They now continued their retreat so rapidly that our army, with the exception of our division, the sixth, and light, were halted for the necessary supplies of provision to come up.

From this until the twenty-seventh we followed them through mountains, harassing their rear, and suffered much fatigue, for during that time we were very ill supplied with rations, at times wanting bread and rum for two days together, and when we did get it, perhaps only half allowance; we were almost always supplied with beef, but it was of that description that there was little nourishment in it. The cattle were brought from Barbary, and often had to travel many hundred miles before they were used, with very little to eat during their journey; the consequence was, that when killed they were nothing more than a mass of emaciated muscle, with a semi-transparent covering of, what would be a perversion of language to call fat—it was more like a coating of train oil. It was never bled properly; and when boiled, it was as tough and stringy as a piece of junk. The water it was boiled in was dignified with the name of soup: and if the blood which boiled out of the beef, along with the wood-ashes that fell into it, constituted soup, we had it in perfection.

One day we had halted rather early; at this time we had been without rations for two days. Many a curse was poured on the head of the commissary, who was considered the responsible person.

"There comes the stores, at last," cried one of the men.

"Where? where?" said those around. Every eye was now directed to a hill at some distance, where a long train of mules were perceived successively rising over its summit, and bending their way towards the division. The men were in transports of joy; a general cheer greeted their appearance.

"We will have full rations today," cried one.

"And rum, too," said another, "for I can see casks on the mules."

Another cheer succeeded this discovery; and we were dancing about overjoyed.

"Who goes for the rations? Get out blankets for the biscuit, and camp-kettles for the rum."

There were soon enough of volunteers for this duty. The mules had by this time got into a sort of defile. Every eye was on the stretch waiting for their reappearance. As the first mule emerged from the place where they were hid, every face was dressed in smiles; but the next second produced an effect, similar to that which a criminal might feel, who had been informed of his reprieve on the scaffold, and the next moment told it was a mistake; for it turned out to be mules with ammunition for the division. Never did I witness such a withering effect on men, as this disappointment produced. We stood looking at each other for a minute, in all the agony of hope deferred: the next was opened by a torrent of execration on all concerned. Those who have never experienced extreme hunger can form no idea of our feelings.

A day or two after this, we crossed a river and ascended a hill, where we encamped. Dennis and I were for duty, and both placed on the out-picket, which was posted on the face of a hill in front of the division. The French were on the opposite rise, and a small river ran at the foot of it. We had only got one day's rations from the time the incident mentioned above occurred; and as Dennis expressed it, "our bellies were thinking our throats were cut."

I procured leave from the officer to go to the river for water; intending to proceed a little farther down, to try if I could find anything that I could eat. Turning round the hill, I came to a mill; and entering it, found a number of soldiers belonging to different regiments of the division, busy grinding Indian corn; others were employed drawing a baking of bread, which the French had left in their hurry, when we took up our position. I attempted to help myself to some corn, which was lying in a basket.

"Drop that like a hot potato," said one of the Connaught Rangers.

I tried another basket, but it was also appropriated; and as there were none of my regiment there, I could not expect to succeed by force; so I left the place, sorrowful enough, on my way back to the picket, with a cargo of cold water—poor cheer, certainly. But just as I turned round the hill, I met my friend Dennis, who had got leave from the officer on some pretence to go down to the river. I told him my melancholy story; he paused for a moment; then clapping his hand to his forehead, he exclaimed, "Now I have it! Give me the canteens!"

When I gave them to him, he poured out the water, and slung them over his shoulder.

"Now, just stand there a minute," said he, "and I'll show you a scatter."

He then commenced running, with the canteens clattering at his back. Those who were in the mill, being startled by the noise, looked out to see what was the matter. When Dennis saw them, he cried out, "Och, ye rogues o' the world, run for your lives; for the division has fell in, and the provost is coming down with his guard; and everyone of yees will be taken."

They were all out in a moment.

"Which way is he coming?"

"This way," said Dennis, pointing' to the way he had come himself. "I am on picket, and I just run down to give you warning."

They all took to their heels in the opposite direction, leaving the field clear to Dennis and me; and we lost no time in filling our haversacks.

The right of the French army had retreated by the high road upon Celerico, but the left (which we were pursuing) had fallen back upon Govea and the mountains of Guarda; and having augmented their force, held the position in great strength.

Our army having collected in the neighbourhood of Celerico, on the morning of the 29th our division moved for the purpose of flanking the enemy, and the light and sixth divisions having moved also, by different routes, in the direction of Guarda, the attack was combined in such a manner that the enemy was nearly surprised, and abandoned many of their effects in their flight, without attempting to fire a shot, notwithstanding the strong position they occupied,[1] and retired on Sabugal on the Coa, leaving an advanced guard on our side.

The position which the enemy had now taken was very strong, the river behind which they were posted being difficult of access, and could only be approached by its left.

Our troops were set in motion on the morning of the 3rd April, to turn the enemy's left above Sabugal, and to force the passage of the bridge of that town. A strong corps of the enemy were posted on a height immediately above the bridge.

The light division and cavalry were ordered to cross the river at two separate fords, upon the enemy's left. The fifth

---

1. Guarda lies on the top of a high hill; we were much fatigued in ascending it, and entered the town with empty stomachs; but we were agreeably surprised to find that the French had left their dinners for us ready cooked, as in their haste they had left them on the fire in the different houses where they had been lodged. In one house where some of their officers were quartered, and had been obliged to retreat from table, after it was laid for dinner, some wag placed a mule's head in the centre, with a label in its mouth on which was written, *"Pour Mons. Jean Bull."*

division and artillery were destined to attack the bridge, and our division to cross at a ford about a mile above the town. The light division crossed first, and commenced the attack, but they were warmly received, and the action was for some time doubtful. Our division now crossed and attacked their centre; while at the same time the fifth division, crossing the bridge, ascended the heights on the right flank of the enemy, and the cavalry appeared in rear of their left; they made a precipitate retreat, leaving a howitzer in possession of the light division, and about two hundred killed on the ground, six officers, and three hundred prisoners.

As we descended the hill towards the river, we passed a convent or chapel, half way down; at the door lay an old man, who had been killed with a musket-shot, and a genteelly dressed Portuguese was standing beside him; he spoke to us as we passed, but we had no time then to pay any attention to what he said. We learned after, from the men who were following us with the baggage, that he had been hung up by some of the French soldiers, because he would not, or could not, show them where he had hid his money. His old father who was lying at the door, had been shot, and his mother's throat cut. His sisters had been first violated by the monsters, and then cruelly used: one of them had her eyes blackened, and the other her arm broken. His life was saved by the French general, who came up just as he had been suspended, and ordered him to be cut down. Such were the tender mercies of the French soldiery!

When we had gained the edge of the river, the French columns were posted on the height above us. We passed the river under a heavy fire, and proceeded to ascend the hill. We could now see that more of our army had crossed, both to our right and left. As we advanced up the hill, we formed line. General Picton rode up in front of us, with his stick over his shoulder, exposed to the heavy fire of the enemy, as composedly as if he had been in perfect safety.

"Steady, my lads, steady!" said he; "don't throw away your fire until I give you the word of command."

We were now close on them; the balls were whizzing about our ears like hailstones. The man before me received a shot in the head, and fell.

"Why don't they let us give the rascals a volley?" said some of the men.

The left of our brigade, which was nearest them, now opened a heavy fire; and by the time the line was all formed, the French had taken to their heels. At this moment a severe rain storm commenced, and darkened the air so much that we lost sight of them completely; when the sky cleared up, they were discovered, about a mile forward, scrambling their way over hedge and ditch without any regularity. The ground which they had occupied now lay before us, strewed with the dead and wounded; and the Portuguese regiment belonging to our division were busy stripping them naked. In this barbarous action, however, they were joined by very few of the British. The division to our right and left had by this time succeeded in turning the flanks of the French army; and they were now retreating in great confusion.

After waiting under arms for some time, we were ordered to encamp on the ground we then occupied, where we remained during that night.

CHAPTER 12

Fuentes de Honore

The night we passed in the encampment at Sabugal was uncommonly dark, and at intervals the rain fell in torrents; fires had been kindled in the hollow trunks of some large chestnut trees, which, burning up as high as the branches, illuminated them to the very top. The flickering lurid glare which these fiery columns threw on the naked bodies of the slain, the indistinct objects in the background, and the groups of soldiers which flitted around them, presented a scene at once sublime and picturesque; it looked like the midnight orgies of some supernatural beings.

Next morning we fell in at daylight, and, in a short time after, pursued our march by the same route the French had taken the preceding day. The ground was covered with gum cistus, which had been previously burned, either through accident, or to serve some purpose, among which they had left visible marks of their confused flight, in the torn pieces of clothing and broken arms which strewed their line of march. They continued their retreat without halting until they reached Ciudade Roderigo, a fortified town on the Spanish frontier, at which place, having crossed the Agueda, they made a stand and concentrated their force. In consequence of this our army also halted, and, in a few days after, our regiment was quartered in a Portuguese village within some miles of them.

On the advance to this place, I became acquainted with a lad of the name of Henry G———. While on guard with him one day, I perceived him reading a book, which, on inquiry, I found to be Cromek's *Remains of Nithsdale and Galloway Song*, which he had borrowed from an officer's servant. Books of any kind were rare amongst us at that time; but one of this description had too much nationality in it, not to be considered a valuable prize in a foreign land. We read the book together, and a similarity of feeling and sentiment subsequently led to a friendship which continued unimpaired while we remained in the Peninsula. In his romantic turn of mind and acute sensibility, he bore a strong resemblance to my former friend and shipmate, William. He had read a great deal, but, like myself, he had read with little discrimination. The effects were nearly the same in both, a propensity to daydreaming and castle-building.

Many a weary mile have we travelled together, almost unconscious of progression, charming the sense of hunger away by anticipating our future honour and preferment, and in forming romantic schemes of rural retirement, when our campaigns were ended. This peculiarity of disposition, although it might sometimes occasion us uneasiness, where others, less sensitive, felt but little, yet, on the whole, in a life like ours, where the scene was continually shifting, it rendered our minds more elastic; and the continual play of fancy which was thus excited, diversified the lights and shadows so much, that even now, I am at a loss to say, whether at that time I felt more pain or pleasure.

We had only been a few days in quarters, when my friend Henry was near being involved in an affair, the consequence of which would have ruined a mind like his forever. The captain of his company was a man of a strange disposition, which rendered him an object of dislike to both officers and men. A fellow of infinite jest, he rarely spoke but in a humorous strain; but there was a "laughing devil in his sneer," and, like the cat, when she has secured her prey, he always felt most inclined to sport with the individual on whose destruction he was bent. It would be endless to enter into a detail of the methods by which he tormented his company—those who served under him will remember them well; suffice it to say, that I have known many officers who possessed bad qualities, but none who possessed fewer good ones than Captain S——.

On the march, he was in the habit of riding his mule among the ranks, very much to the annoyance of his company, and one day during the previous advance, the column was marching through fields which were fenced in by broad thin stones. The other officers finding they could not get through conveniently with the regiment, had taken a lane to the right of the column, but he continued to move on; finding, however, that his mule could not get through the openings made, he desired Henry to overturn one of the stones. Henry made the attempt, but finding his strength inadequate to the task, and seeing himself getting behind the regiment, he passed through and rejoined his company.

The captain had now to take the same road with the other officers. When he overtook the column, foaming with rage, he commenced in a measured affected style, to abuse Henry, ending with his usual phrase of encouragement, *"I'll get you a sweet five hundred."* From that day forward, poor Henry was marked out as a butt for his caprice and tyranny. Not long after, two men of the company were ordered to be confined on a charge of selling their necessaries, one of whom happened to be Henry's comrade, and Captain S—— thinking this a favourable opportunity for carrying his promise into effect, ordered him to be confined, also. A court-martial was ordered, and the prisoners warned for trial. Whether by some sinister manoeuvring, or that it fell his regular turn, Captain S—— was president.

The witnesses were examined; the evidence was sufficiently clear against the other two, but none was adduced against Henry.

The president, trusting, I suppose, to his influence with the other members, proceeded (without taking any notice of the total want of evidence against Henry) to recommend the prisoners to acknowledge the crime laid to their charge, and throw themselves on the mercy of the court. Poor Henry was so struck with the flagrant injustice of this proceeding, that he could scarcely muster courage sufficient to say that he had heard no evidence against him. The president did not allow him to finish what he had to say, before he opened on him with a string of the most abusive epithets; and then, addressing himself to the members of the court—

"Gentlemen," said he, "this is one of the most insolent dogs in my company. You may take my word for it, he is guilty—he confessed to me that he was, before I confined him, which I can prove."

The members sat mute, as is generally the case while under the influence of a superior officer's rhetoric; and Henry had bade farewell to hope, when one of the officers, who was but a young subaltern, bursting through the blind deference too often cringingly paid to power, even in matters where discipline is not concerned, and giving way to the words which a natural love of justice prompted—

"We have no right, Captain S——," said he, "sitting here as we do, to try the case according to the evidence laid before us, to presume that the prisoner is guilty, in the absence of all evidence. Nor are we entitled to pay attention to any representation which you may feel inclined to make, prejudicial to his character. Sitting where you do as president of this court—either sufficient evidence must be produced against the prisoner, or we are bound to acquit him."

Captain S—— turned the scowl of his dark grey eyes upon him, wherein the disappointment of baffled revenge and rage were distinctly visible: but the subaltern bore the look intended for his annihilation with the utmost indifference—there even seemed to be a smile of contempt playing on his countenance. Captain S—— then proceeded to bring forward evidence to prove Henry's connexion with the crime for which the prisoners were tried principally for the purpose of proving that he had confessed his guilt; and, according to the president's opinion, this evidence was perfectly conclusive.

The officer already mentioned, seeing that Henry was nearly sinking under the influence of his feelings, said, "Don't be afraid,

my man, justice will be done you—I believe you to be innocent—at least, I have heard nothing yet to induce me to think
otherwise; take time, collect yourself, and if you have any questions to ask the evidence, or any witnesses to call in your defence, to disprove what has been stated, speak out fearlessly."

Encouraged by the officer's kind and manly conduct, and
with his assistance, Henry cross-questioned the evidence, and
brought forward witnesses that not only disproved all that had
been stated against him, but fixed a suspicion on the minds of
those present, that the president had not only confined him
without cause, but had suborned witnesses for the purpose of
bringing him to punishment.

Captain S—— seeing that his designs were frustrated, sul-
lenly gave up the point, and poor Henry was acquitted; but had
it not been for the independent character of the officer above-
mentioned, he might not have escaped punishment.

Courts-martial were at that time much too frequent to expect that justice would be always administered impartially by
them; and I am sorry to say, it was too often evident that individual pique influenced the decisions. In some regiments, indeed, courts-martial were resorted to, merely to give a colour
to the proceedings of the officer commanding, whose wishes
were oftener consulted than the ends of justice. This was not
remedied by what are called company courts-martial, where
the individual was tried by his peers; for I remember in one
case, where I was president, the point in agitation among the
members was not, "What punishment was adequate to the
crime?" but "What punishment would please the commanding
officer?" and I had some difficulty in convincing them that the
former was the point they had to determine. The surveillance,
established by the commander-in-chief over courts-martial,
was a wise measure, and has altered matters very much. Indeed,
too much praise cannot be bestowed for the humane and effective policy which has been gradually introduced into the
army: the situation of the soldier at present is very different
from what it was twenty years ago. From the specimen Henry

had got of Captain S——'s disposition, he thought it the wisest plan to get transferred from his company, which he effected shortly after.

A few days after this occurrence, our regiment was moved to the village of Fuentes de Honore, a few miles nearer Almeida: great part of the way, we moved through a wood of oak trees, in which the inhabitants of the surrounding villages had herds of swine feeding: here the voice of the cuckoo never was mute; night and day its simple notes were heard in every quarter of the wood.

The village we now occupied was in Spain, and formed a striking contrast to those of Portugal; the inhabitants and their houses wore an air of neatness, cleanliness, and comfort about them, unlike anything we had as yet seen in the country; their dress and language were also different.

The site of the village itself was beautiful and romantic; it lay in a sort of ravine, down which a small river brawled over an irregular rocky bed, in some places forming precipitous falls of many feet; the acclivity on each side was occasionally abrupt, covered with trees and thick brushwood. Three leagues to the left of our front lay the villages of Gallegos and Espeja, in and about which our light division and cavalry were quartered. Between this and Fuentes lay a large wood, which, receding on the right, formed a plain, flanked by a deep ravine, being a continuation of that in which the village lay; in our rear was another plain, (on which our army subsequently formed,) and behind that, in a valley, Villa Formosa, the river Coa running past it.

We had not been many days here, when we received intelligence that the light troops were falling back upon our village, the enemy having recrossed the Agueda in great force, for the purpose of relieving Almeida, which we had blockaded. On the morning we received this intelligence, (the 3rd of May, 1811,) our regiment turned out of the town, and took up their position with the rest of the division on a plain, some distance behind it. The morning was uncommonly beautiful, the sun shone bright and warm, the various odoriferous shrubs, which were scattered profusely around, perfumed the air, and the woods rang with the songs of birds. The light division and cavalry falling back, followed by the columns of the French, the various divisions of the army assembling on the plain from different quarters, their arms glittering in the sun, bugles blowing, drums beating, the various staff officers galloping about to different parts of the line giving orders, formed a scene which realized to my mind all that I had ever read of feats of arms, or the pomp of war; a scene which no one could behold unmoved, or without feeling a portion of that enthusiasm which always accompanies "deeds of high daring;" a scene justly conceived and well described by Moore, in the beautiful song:

Oh the sight entrancing,
When morning's beam is glancing
O'er files arrayed,
With helm and blade,
And plumes in the gay wind dancing.

Our position was now taken up in such a way, that our line ran along the frontiers of Portugal, maintaining the blockade of Almeida by our left, while our right kept open the communication with Sabugal, the place where the last action was fought.

The French advanced on our position in three columns, about three o'clock in the afternoon, and detached a strong body of troops against Fuentes, which was at this time occupied as an advanced post by the 60th regiment, and the light company of our division. The skirmishers were covered in their advance by cavalry, in consequence of which ours were obliged to fall back, for greater safety, to some stone fences on the outskirts of the village, while a party of our German hussars covered their retreat. The cavalry now commenced skirmishing, the infantry keeping up an occasional fire. It was rather remarkable that the cavalry on both sides happened to be Germans.

When this was understood, volleys of insulting language, as well as shot, were exchanged between them. One of our hussars got so enraged at something one of his opponents said, that raising his sword, he dashed forward upon him into the very centre of their line. The French hussar, seeing that he had no mercy to expect from his enraged foe, wheeled about his horse, and rode to the rear; the other, determined on revenge, still continued to follow him. The whole attention of both sides was drawn for a moment to these two, and a temporary cessation of firing took place; the French staring in astonishment at our hussar's temerity, while our men were cheering him on.

The chase continued for some way to the rear of their cavalry. At last our hussar coming up with him, and fetching a furious blow, brought him to the ground. Awakening now to a sense of the danger he had thrown himself into, he set his horse at full speed to get back to his comrades; but the French, who were confounded when he passed, had recovered their surprise, and determined on revenging the death of their comrade; they joined in pursuit, firing their pistols at him. The poor fellow was now in a hazardous plight; they were every moment gaining upon him, and he had still a long way to ride.

A band of the enemy took a circuit, for the purpose of intercepting him; and before he could reach the line he was surrounded, and would have been cut in pieces, had not a party of his comrades, stimulated by the wish to save so brave a fellow, rushed forward, and just arrived in time, by making the attack general, to save his life, and brought him off in triumph.

The overwhelming force which the French now pushed forward on the village, could not be withstood by the small number of troops which defended it; they were obliged to give way, and were fairly forced to a rising ground on the other side, where stood a small chapel. The French now thought they had gained their point, but they were soon undeceived; for being reinforced at this place by the Portuguese cacadores, our lads came to the right about, and attacked them with such vigour, that in a short time they were driven back to their old ground.

While retreating through the town, one of our sergeants who had run up the wrong street, being pushed hard by the enemy, ran into one of the houses: they were close at his heels; and he had just time to tumble himself into a large chest, and let the lid down, when they entered and commenced plundering the house, expressing their wonder at the same time concerning the sudden disappearance of the *"Anglois,"* whom they had seen run into the house. During the time, the poor sergeant lay sweating, and half smothered; they were busy breaking up every tiling that came in their way, looking for plunder; and they were in the act of opening the lid of his hiding-place, when the noise of our men cheering, as they charged the enemy through the town, forced them to take to flight. He now got out, and having joined his company, assisted in driving the French back.

No other part of the line had as yet been attacked by the French; they seemed bent on taking the village of Fuentes in the first place, as a "stepping-stone," and the main body of each army lay looking at each other. Finding that the force they had sent down, great as it was, could not keep possession of the place, they sent forward two strong bodies of fresh troops to retake it, one of which, composed of the Irish legion, dressed in red uniform, was at first taken for a British regiment, and they had time to form up, and give us a volley before the mistake was discovered. The village was now vigorously attacked by the enemy at two points, and with such a superior force, that in spite of the unparalleled bravery of our troops, they were driven back contesting every inch of the ground.

On our retreat through the village, we were met by the 71st regiment, cheering, led on by Colonel Cadogan; which had been detached from the line to our support. The chase was now turned, and although the French were obstinately intent on keeping their ground, and so eager, that many of their cavalry had entered the town, and rushed furiously down the streets, all their efforts were in vain: nothing could withstand the charge of the gallant 71st; and in a short time, in spite of all resistance, they cleared the village. This regiment during the Peninsular War, was always remarkable for its gallantry. The brave Cadogan well knew the art of rendering his men invincible; he knew that the courage of the British soldier is best called forth by associating it with his country, and he also knew how to time the few words which produced such magical effects. We were now once more in possession of the place, but our loss, as well as that of the French, had been very great.

In particular places of the village, where a stand had been made, or the shot brought to bear, the slaughter had been immense, which was the case near the river, and at the small chapel on our side of the town; among the rest lay one poor fellow of the 88th light company, who had been severely wounded, and seemed to suffer excruciating agony, for he begged of those who passed him to put him out of torture. Although from the nature of his wound there was no possibility of his surviving, yet none felt inclined to comply with his request, until a German of the 60th rifle battalion, after hesitating a few moments, raised his rifle, and putting the muzzle of it to his head fired the contents of it through it. Whether this deed deserved praise or blame, I leave others to determine.

The French, enraged at being thus baffled in all their attempts to take the town, sent forward a force composed of the very flower of their army; but they gained only a temporary advantage, for being reinforced by the 79th regiment, although the contest remained doubtful until night, we remained in possession of it, with the exception of a few houses on the rise of the hill at the French side.

The light brigade of our division was now withdrawn, and the 71st and 79th regiments remained as a picket in it during the night; next morning it was again occupied as before.

On the fourth, both sides were busily employed burying the dead and bringing in the wounded; French and English promiscuously mixed, and assisted each other in that melancholy duty as if they had been intimate friends. So far did this friendship extend, that two of our lads who spoke French, went up that night after dark to the enemy's picket, and having conversed and drank wine with them, returned unmolested to their company. During this day the French generals reconnoitred our position, and next morning, (the 5th) they made a movement to their left with two strong columns; this caused a corresponding movement in our line, and it was scarcely made, when they attacked our right, composed of the seventh division, with all their cavalry, and succeeded in turning it; but they were gallantly met by some squadrons of our dragoons, and repulsed. Their columns of infantry still continued to advance on the same point, and were much galled by the heavy fire kept up on them by the seventh division; but in consequence of this movement, our communication with Sabugal was abandoned for a stronger position, and our army was now formed in two lines, the light division and cavalry in reserve; this manoeuvre paralysed their attack on our line, and their efforts were now chiefly confined to partial cannonading, and some charges with their cavalry, which were received and repulsed by the pickets of the first division in one instance; but as they were falling back, they did not perceive the charge of a different body in time to form, and many of them were killed, wounded, and taken prisoners. Colonel Hill, who commanded the pickets, was among the latter; the 42nd regiment also, under Lord Blantyre, gallantly repulsed another charge made by the enemy's cavalry. The French then attempted to push a strong body of light infantry down the ravine to the right of the first division, but they were driven back by some companies of the guards and 95th rifles.

While on the right this was going on, the village of Fuentes was again attacked by a body of the Imperial Guard, and, as on the third, the village was taken and retaken several times. At one time they had brought down such an overwhelming force, that our troops were fairly beat out of the town, and the French formed close column between it and us; some guns which were posted on the rise in front of our line, having opened upon them, made them change their ground; and the 88th regiment (Connaught Rangers) being detached from our division, led on by the heroic General McKinnon (who commanded our right brigade,) charged them furiously, and drove them back through the village with great slaughter.

Some time previous to this, General Picton had had occasion to check this regiment for some plundering affair they had been guilty of, and he was so offended at their conduct, that in addressing them, he had told them they were the greatest blackguards in the army—but as he was always as ready to give praise as censure, where it was due, when they were returning from this gallant and effective charge, he exclaimed, " Well done the brave 88th!"

Some of them, who had been stung at his former reproaches, cried out, "Are we the greatest blackguards in the army now?"

The valiant Picton smiled, and replied, "No, no, you are brave and gallant soldiers; this day has redeemed your character."

At one time during the contest, when the enemy had gained a partial possession of the village, our light troops had retired into a small wood above it, where they were huddled together without any regularity; a French officer, while leading on his men, having been killed in our front, a bugler of the 83rd regiment starting out between the fire of both parties, seized his gold watch; but he had scarcely returned, when a cannon-shot from the enemy came whistling past him, and he fell lifeless on the spot. The blood started out of his nose and ears, but with the exception of this, there was neither wound nor bruise on his body; the shot had not touched him. The phenomenon here described has been the subject of much discussion among medical men, some attributing it to the shot becoming electrical and parting with its electricity in passing the body; while others maintain, that the ball does strike the individual obliquely, and although there is no appearance of injury on the surface, there always exists serious derangement of the system internally.

We had regained possession of the village a short time after, and got a little breathing time; a few of our lads and some of the 79th were standing together, where a poor fellow lay a few paces from them weltering in his blood. As he belonged to the 79th, they went over to see who he was; the ball had entered the centre of his forehead, and passed through his brain, and to all appearance he was completely dead; but when any of the flies which were buzzing about the wound, entered it, a convulsive tremor shook his whole body, and the muscles of his face became frightfully distorted; there could scarcely be imagined anything more distressing, or more appalling to the spectator.

Within the walls of the old chapel, where our men and the French had got under cover alternately, as they were pursuing or pursued, there lay a mixture of various nations, wounded, dying, and dead, and presented a sight which no language could describe, raving, groaning, calling for assistance and drink. He must have had a hardened heart who could have beheld it without feeling deeply. One noble-looking fellow of the Imperial Guard lay wounded through both legs, and one of his arms shattered; he had been plundered and stripped half naked. One of our light company, of the name of James Cochran, as much distinguished for bravery in the field as for a mild and humane temper, (for they are not incompatible,) seeing the poor fellow lying in this plight, unable to help himself, and the flies irritating his wounds—threw his own blanket over him—brought some water, and left it and some bread with him; but what was his mortification on returning that way, to find that he was again plundered of all, and left as before. The poor fellow, however, seemed to feel the most lively gratitude for what Cochran had done, and wished to force some money on him, which had escaped the search of his plunderers.

After the various taking and retaking of the village, night again found us in possession of it. On the 6th no attempt was made to renew the attack, and, as on the 4th, the army on each side were employed in burying the dead, and looking after the wounded. On the 7th we still remained quiet: but on this day the whole French army were reviewed on the plain by Massena. On the night of the 7th, some companies of our regiment were detached on picket to the ravine on the left of the town, and during the night I was placed one of the outpost sentries. The French pickets occupied the opposite side, and the distance between us was trifling. The night was very dark, and the place where I was posted was amongst bushes and trees, near the river's edge. All was still, save the river, gurgling over its rocky bed, or when a slight breeze set the leaves in motion, and the *qui vive* of the French sentinels could be distinctly heard.

I had been some time posted, ruminating on the awful responsibility attached to my post, as it was probable the enemy might make an attack during the night. I was straining my eyes through the thick darkness towards the spot where I imagined the French sentry was placed, at the same time eagerly listening. In the midst of this anxiety I was alarmed by the noise of something rustling among the bushes near the river. The thought struck me instantly that it must be the French picket advancing on my post; my first impulse was to fire in the direction of the noise, but I recollected that there was a possibility of giving a false alarm, and I felt myself in a strange dilemma—I could not fire until I ascertained that it was an enemy, and before that could be done I might be surprised and killed.

The noise ceased, but still I was all attention, for this did not give me confidence; sticking my ramrod in the ground, I put my ear to it, but could hear nothing. I now assumed more courage, and almost persuaded myself I had been deceived. At that moment, a burst through the bushes in my front, accompanied by a horrid yell, robbed me of all presence of mind. In the desperation which fear sometimes inspires, I dashed forward against the object of my alarm with my charged bayonet, and plunged it in the foe; he fell, and for a few seconds I had not power to move. Silence was now only broken by the smothered groan of my dying victim; and recovering myself a little, I stooped to ascertain whether it was really a French grenadier I had slain, but found it was only a poor ass's colt which had strayed from its dam, and browsing about had thus been the unconscious cause of my alarm.

On the 8th the French sentries were withdrawn at daylight, the main body of the enemy having retired during the night, to the woods between Fuentes and Gallejos. On the 9th they broke up, and retired from their position; and on the 10th they had recrossed the Agueda without having accomplished the relief of Almeida. On the morning of the 11th, however, about one o'clock, a.m. the garrison having blown up part of the fortifications, made their escape past the troops who had blockaded them, in consequence of the darkness of the night—some said the carelessness of the regiments on that duty. One regiment in particular was blamed, but the excuse might be more properly sought for in the masterly dispositions which the governor (General Brenier) had made, both for the escape of the garrison, and the subsequent retreat.

CHAPTER 13
Failure at Badajoz

We were again quartered in Fuentes, but the place was sadly altered; the inhabitants had fled, many of the houses were destroyed, and all of them plundered; although the dead had been in general buried, there still remained some bodies lying about swelled and blackened by the heat of the sun; the ground was strewed with uniform caps and clothing, and the streets were dyed with the blood of the combatants; the whole place wore an air of desolation and wretchedness. We were only a few days there when we received orders to march along with the 7th division, for the purpose of laying siege to Badajos, a fortified town on the Spanish frontier, in the province of Estremadura. The distance between Fuentes and Badajos might be about forty leagues, Portuguese, (one hundred and fifty miles;) we proceeded by Alfeyates, Penamacore, and Castello Branco, where we were quartered in a Franciscan convent for two days.

From thence we marched to Villa Valhe, where boats were ready for us to cross the Tagus. This was a romantic spot: the side on which we lay previous to passing was a plain, the opposite one a mountain, which rose abrupt and precipitous, clothed with trees and bushes to the top, throwing its dark shade on the bosom of the river, which rolled along at its base, deep, dark, and rapid.

Here it was reported Lord Wellington had lost his two orderly dragoons some days before. He had received information that the French army under Marshal Soult was coming down in great force on Beresford's army, and he was so anxious to get forward, that when he came to the river, and found the bridge of boats not thrown across, he plunged in, followed by his orderly dragoons, (certainly a most hazardous attempt;) the current was so strong that the dragoons with their horses were carried away and drowned, his lordship only escaping by the superior strength of his horse.

Having crossed the river, we proceeded by a winding road cut in the face of the hill to Niza; this was a most distressing march, being up hill the whole way. Passing Alpalhao, we reached Porto Legre two days after. From this we marched to Arronches, and from thence to Campo Mayor, situated about ten miles from Badajos, where we remained for some days, while preparations were making for the siege. This was a very handsome town, walled, but very slightly fortified; one building in particular, a small chapel, called Capella des Ossos, is worth noticing. It had been erected to commemorate some massacre. The whole interior was built up with skulls and thigh bones, laid across, and two skeletons, one on each side, were built into the wall.

On the 25th of May we marched towards Badajos, which the French had gained possession of in the beginning of the campaign, through the treachery of the Spanish governor, at the very time Lord Wellington had promised relief, and given orders to hold out. When we first came in sight of the town, its spires appeared above the hill which rises on the Campo Mayor side of it, as if the town lay immediately beneath, but we found it was still a great way off; we then took a circuitous route to the left of the town, and having crossed the Guidiana, we encamped about three miles from it, on the slope of a small hill which skirted the Elvas road; here we constructed huts in the best manner we could, with bushes and branches of trees.

On the night of the 29th, the stores and ordnance having arrived, we marched down towards the town, for the purpose of breaking ground: it was fortunately very dark, and as we kept the greatest silence, the French were not aware of our approach. When we reached the place where it was intended we should open the trenches, we formed a line across the front of the town, where two thousand entrenching tools had been laid. We were then told our safety depended on expedition, for if the French discovered our presence before we had worked ourselves under cover, a warm salute might be expected.

The officers were dependent on our exertions for safety; and it was remarked in what kind and familiar tones some of these spoke, who, in greater security, would have acted the blustering tyrant. I cannot understand what makes many officers so supercilious, haughty, and morose to their men, when, by a little good humour, or friendly feeling displayed, I have no doubt they might not only make themselves beloved, but have their orders much better obeyed.

We now commenced work vigorously, and in six hours were under cover, without the French having discovered our presence. The operations of the siege were now carried on with great vigour on both sides of the river Guidiana; the opposite one was conducted by the seventh division against fort St Christoval, an outwork that protected the advance to the bridge. By the 2nd of June we had two batteries playing on the walls, and four were opened by the seventh division on fort St. Christoval. The guns were partly served by Portuguese artillery, who behaved extremely well. The troops were told off in two parties, relieving each other every twenty-four hours.

A communication was kept up between the several trenches, and a covered way formed, which prevented the men from being so much exposed in going to, and returning from the camp; but still we suffered severely from the enemy's shot and shell, with which they now plied us hotly, having their guns constantly ready to fire at even a single individual if he put his head above the trench; and the shells fired from the garrison were thrown so as to make them fall in it. At night we could see them by the fuse, and were often enabled to get out of their way; in the day, we ran more risk, although we could still distinguish them from shot, by the whistling sound they made coming through the air.

The second or third night after the trenches were opened,

Dennis and I were down on the working party. Captain S——, already mentioned, was one of the officers. They were telling off a covering party, who were to go out in front, to prevent any sudden surprise by the enemy making a sortie, when the word "shell!" was given. All eyes were instantly turned on it, watching its direction, that they might run in the opposite one. Captain S——, although so valiant on parade, seemed to have no predilection for a "glorious death" more than his neighbours; and he, in company with a brother captain, headed the retreat. They had not gone many paces, when notice was given of another shell falling in the direction they were running. By this time the first had fallen short of the trench, and a retrograde movement took place; but the captains were now in a bad plight, for the crowd was so condensed in the direction they had to go, that there was no getting through.

The shell was giving intelligence by its quickened revolutions, that it was falling, but there was no means of escape, the whole were fairly wedged in and had fallen on each other; and had the shell burst among them, it would have made dreadful havoc. As I threw myself down by the side of the trench, I perceived Captain S—— running about like a chicken in a coop, seeking an opening by which he might escape, but finding none, he wormed his head into the crowd, which had fallen in his front, and thus remained. The shell fell in a direction that placed me in imminent danger; but I could not refrain from laughing at his ludicrous position; it burst, however, without doing any injury.

On one occasion, when Dennis and I were on duty in the trench, and at one of the batteries with some others, at the formation of an embrasure, we had nearly completed it, but it still required opening and facing off towards the enemy; this was a very hazardous business, as we were sure of a volley of cannon-shot the moment we mounted the parapet.

"Come, my brave fellows," said the superintending engineer officer, "which of you will volunteer to go outside, and form the embrasure?"

Dennis and I were standing close by him, and jumped upon the top of the breastwork. We were followed by two more, but had scarcely appeared when a cannon-shot striking the parapet close to where I stood, covered me with earth.

"Never mind," said Dennis, "to miss is as good as a mile." He scarcely had finished, when he was served in the same manner—no way dispirited, he exclaimed, "Time about is fair play." One of the lads who worked with us began to show symptoms of fear, "Don't be afraid," said Dennis, "you'll never die till your time come." His eloquence did not seem to take effect. "Go into the trench," said Dennis, "we will do without you." The lad was in the act of doing so, when a shot struck him, and he fell mortally wounded.

Soon after, our dinners having come down, we were relieved by others, and called in. The mess I belonged to had sat down round the camp kettle, and were beginning to help themselves, when the cry "shell!" was given; all were to their feet in an instant, for we found by the noise that it was coming in our direction. The others endeavoured to make their escape; whether from a belief in Dennis's doctrine of predestination, I cannot at present recollect; but, instead of running from it, I threw myself down flat in the embrasure. I had scarcely done so, when the shell fell within two yards of me.

"Now," thought I, "there is no chance of escape;" and during the few seconds of suspense, while the last part of the fuse was whizzing in my ear, reflections which would have occupied an hour at another time, on home, parents, death, and my future fate, whirled through my mind, like a wild and giddy dream. The shell burst, and for a few moments I was bereaved of recollection. Coming to myself, I scrambled out from amongst the stuff with which I was covered.

"Are you kilt?" asked Dennis, running up to me with an expression of real concern.

Looking to myself to see whether I was wounded, I replied, " No;" but I had been well frightened.

"That's right, my boy," said he, "I don't believe the shot's made that will kill any of us. Many's the long yarn about this business I'll be after telling to the ould women of Ireland yet."

On the sixth, the breach in fort St. Christoval being considered practicable, a detachment of the different regiments composing the seventh division was selected to storm it: being at night we could not see the attack farther than the flash of their firearms, which, from our encampment, looked like an exhibition of fire-works; but we understood that from the nature of the impediments thrown in the way, although they had advanced under a heavy discharge of shot and shell from the town, and musketry and hand grenades from the garrison, they were unable to succeed, and ordered to retire.

The firing was continued upon the breach for three days longer, and a second attempt was made to carry it on the evening of the ninth, with another detachment of the seventh division. The attack was made with the utmost gallantry, and they advanced intrepidly to the foot of the breach; but the same obstacles presented themselves as on the first attempt, and after having suffered most severely, without being able to effect a lodgement, they were again ordered to retire. The loss in officers and men was considerable.

The men of our division, unaccustomed to failure in any enterprise, and perhaps rather conceited, were inclined to attribute the failure of these attempts to the troops composing the seventh division being mostly foreigners; but in this opinion it is likely they were wrong, as in the subsequent storming of the town, in the ensuing year, the obstacles thrown in the way were sufficient to resist even the bravest British troops. A day or two after this affair, intelligence having been received that Soult was advancing with a large army, for the purpose of relieving Badajos, Wellington deemed it prudent to raise the siege, converting it into a blockade.

From this until the seventeenth we were busy withdrawing the guns and stores, which were sent to the garrison of Elvas, as a place of security, and on the seventeenth quitted our investment of the place, and withdrew to Campo Mayor. On the morning we left it, the French cavalry were out skirmishing with a party of the eleventh hussars, who were covering our retreat, and followed us the greater part of the way.

While in Campo Mayor, where we remained for some time, a German of the sixtieth regiment, a Frenchman, and two Italians, belonging to the Chasseurs Britannique, were shot for desertion—the former belonging to our division, the latter three to the seventh. On the morning that the sentence of the first was carried into execution, the division was assembled outside of the town, where they formed three sides of a square. The prisoner was marched past the various regiments, accompanied by the chaplain of the division, and the guard appointed to shoot him. When his devotions were finished, he was blindfolded by the provost-marshal, and placed kneeling on the brink of his grave already open to receive him. He gave the signal, and the next moment he fell pierced by half a dozen musket-balls. The different regiments then marched past the body, receiving the word "eyes left" as they passed him.

I was on the general provost guard the evening previous to those of the seventh division being shot. The sergeants came with the company's books to settle their accounts; the two Italians were in paroxysms of agony, crying and wringing their hands. The behaviour of the Frenchman, who had been taken prisoner, had volunteered into the Chasseurs Britannique, and afterwards deserted from them to his countrymen, formed a strong contrast to that of the others.

Calm and dignified, he seemed to feel no fear of death, nor did any complaint pass his lips, save an occasional exclamation against the injustice of trying him as a deserter, being a Frenchman. In his circumstances, he argued it was natural that he should endeavour to join his friends the first opportunity that offered. When the sergeant was settling their accounts, the Italians paid no attention to anything said to them; but he discussed every item with the greatest exactness, and the sergeant wanting a small coin about the value of a farthing to balance, he desired him to procure it before he would sign the ledger; but though thus exact with the sergeant, the moment he received his balance, which amounted to some dollars, he divided every penny of it amongst his fellow-prisoners.

When the Italians received their money, they sent for brandy, and began to drink intemperately, endeavouring to drown their sorrows and sear their minds; but it had quite a different effect, for they then broke from all restraint in the expression of their feelings, and cried and groaned with agony in such a manner, that they could be heard at a considerable distance from the guard-room. In this state they continued until morning, when they ceased their lamentations, only because nature was exhausted by their former violence.

Quite different was the conduct of the Frenchman: when the brandy was procured, the Italians pressed him to take some, but he thanked them, and refused, "No," said he, throwing a look of mingled pity and contempt on them, "I need no brandy to enable me to face death."

He continued to walk about with his arms folded during the whole evening, without seeming in the least disturbed; occasionally, indeed, his countenance softened, and a teardrop gathered in his eye, but it was not permitted to linger there; and as if ashamed of showing the least want of firmness, he assumed redoubled inflexibility of countenance.

I could not help admiring his manly fortitude and courage. I had no opportunity of speaking to him, without being intrusive; but in silence I watched the expression of his face, with a feeling I could hardly describe. It was reported that he was a brother of Marshal Soult: the truth of this I cannot pretend to affirm. He was, however, certainly a man of a noble mind and independent spirit. About midnight he lay down and slept soundly until near the hour of execution; his courage seemed to be now even more exalted. He washed and dressed himself with the greatest nicety, conversed with his fellow-prisoners cheerfully, and endeavoured, although without success, to infuse some courage into the poor Italians.

The guard having arrived, he took leave of those prisoners

who were confined with him; and to one, with whom he was more familiar than the others, he gave some private injunction, and on parting with him he said emphatically, "Remember, I die a Frenchman."

He marched off to the place of execution with the same collected intrepidity he had before evinced, and I understood afterwards, that his demeanour on the ground where he was shot, was similar to that displayed while a prisoner. All admired his courage, and were sorry for his fate.

CHAPTER 14

Ciudade Roderigo

Leaving Campo Mayor we returned by the same route that we had come, recrossing the Tagus at Ville Valhe and halting at Albergeria, a village near the place from whence we had first set out to go to Badajos, and not far distant from Ciudade Roderigo, in which the French had a garrison.

We remained here in camp for some time, very busy making fascines and gabions to fortify the position which our army had taken. While we lay in this encampment, the weather was uncommonly warm, and the bushes and long grass, among which we had raised temporary huts, were rendered inflammable as tinder; the grass on our left had been by accident set fire to, and the flames soon spread in every direction. The whole of the soldiers were turned out to stop its progress; but in spite of their endeavours, it communicated to a wood which lay on the face of a steep hill in our rear, burning with the greatest fury. The night happened to be very dark, and there could scarcely be anything more grand or awful: the whole mountain was in a blaze of fire, and the noise and crackling of the trees burning was like the noise of a hurricane; it was a scene which a person could stand and gaze at in mute astonishment, without being able to define the sensations which were raised in his mind. The wind fortunately carried the fire to the rear of our encampment, or it might have been productive of great injury, by blowing up the ammunition, &c.

From this place we removed more in advance to Robleda,

a Spanish village. The people seemed to be comfortable, the houses were extremely clean, and here we had a fair specimen of the manners of the Spanish peasantry. All their domestic concerns were conducted with the greatest regularity: they were very punctual in the observance of all the rites of their church, and in catechising their children. They seemed to me to be really pious, and from their prudent industrious habits, happy and contented.

The people I was quartered on were uncommonly friendly; being able to speak the language a little, and Dennis being of the same religious persuasion, we were almost considered as members of the family. The inhabitants were mostly all employed in agriculture, and were very lively and fond of amusement, particularly of singing and dancing; here they had their fandangos and boleros every Sunday evening after mass, dressed in the gay and becoming fashion of their country, and many a ditty was chaunted in praise of General Mina and Don Julian. The village, however, proved very unhealthy: during the short time we were in it, eighty or ninety of our men left us to go to the rear sick, most of them with fever and ague, and among the number my poor friend Dennis.

On the 24th September, in consequence of the advance of the French, we were ordered to march from this to El Bodon; and it was with unfeigned regret on both sides, I believe, that we parted with our friendly hosts.

On the 25th, at two o'clock in the morning, we were turned out to the heights above the town, which our brigade, along with one of cavalry, occupied. Our position was on a range of heights, over which passed the road leading from Roderigo to Fuente Guinaldo. Here we lay under arms until about eight o'clock in the morning, when we perceived, issuing out of Roderigo, one column of cavalry after another, advancing along the road towards our post, to the number of about forty squadrons; these were succeeded by twelve or fourteen battalions of infantry, with twelve pieces of cannon. Our situation now began to get precarious, being completely separated from the rest of the army, by at least six miles. Still we had no orders to retreat—and to retreat without orders is not the custom of the British army.

One of the regiments was posted on the hill over which the road passed, and when it was seen that the French were bent upon advancing in that direction, two more regiments, the 17th British, 21st Portuguese, and the brigade of cavalry, were sent to reinforce them.

This was scarcely done, when the advanced squadrons of the enemy's cavalry and artillery made a furious attack on this post, and succeeded in taking two pieces of Portuguese cannon. The Portuguese artillery behaved bravely, having stood until actually cut down at their guns, which were posted on a rising ground to the right. The 5th regiment was now ordered to charge, and they succeeded in retaking the guns. While this was going on on the right, we were attacked by another body of cavalry in front, which was met and repulsed with determined bravery by the 77th regiment. Our cavalry also were warmly engaged, and charged different bodies of the enemy which ascended on the left.

Here we kept our post gallantly, surrounded by about two thousand cavalry—until at last the French infantry being brought up, we were ordered to retreat in squares on Fuente Guinaldo, supported only by the small body of cavalry already mentioned. The French cavalry seeing us preparing for retreat, rushed furiously on, and the various squares were now successively charged by powerful masses of their cavalry, one in particular on three faces of the square, but they halted, and repulsed them with the utmost steadiness and gallantry.

The French in those charges suffered severely, having a tremendous fire poured in on them each time. As they rushed on with impetuosity, when they were brought to a dead stop by the points of our bayonets, they were thrown into the greatest confusion, and were brought down by our shot in numbers. The whole now proceeded to retreat in excellent order, at an ordinary pace, keeping exact distances, ready to form up in the event of a charge being made.

We were much annoyed by shot and shell from the heights where the French artillery were posted, some of which falling in the squares did great mischief, killing and wounding several of our men, and blowing up our ammunition. We had about six miles to retreat in this manner before we reached the body of the army, with the French cavalry hanging on our flanks and rear, some of whom had even the audacity to ride to our front, and having taken part of our baggage, brought it back close past our columns: we could render no assistance, as our own safety wholly depended on keeping ourselves ready to form square. Here General Picton showed that coolness and intrepidity for which he was so much distinguished; for some time he rode at the head of our square, while a strong body of French hung on our right, waiting a favourable opportunity to charge. The captain who commanded us (both field-officers being sick) was throwing many a fearful glance at them, and was rather in a state of perturbation—"Never mind the French," said Picton "mind your regiment; if the fellows come here, we will give them a warm reception."

At length we came in sight of the rest of our army, and the main body of the French hung back, but we were escorted into the very lines by their advanced guard. Here, however, they met with a warm reception from some squadrons of our cavalry, which made them retreat. We halted in rear of Fuente Guinaldo, where an entrenched camp had been formed, and remained here that night and next day, during which the French, having brought forward their infantry, took post on a hill opposite, and we expected an engagement; but Lord Wellington, for good reasons, no doubt, deemed it more prudent to retire.

When night came, we were ordered to kindle a great number of fires, for the purpose of making the French believe we still remained in our encampment. Two hours after, we commenced our retreat, leaving the fires burning brightly, and marched all night; the road we travelled was uncommonly narrow, and various impediments in the way often caused the rear to halt. The fatigue we had undergone the preceding two or three days, and the almost total want of sleep during that time, completely overcame us; the moment a halt was made, we dropped down on the ground fast asleep, and it was by the greatest exertion that we were able to rouse ourselves to proceed. So overpowering was its effects, that I would have been content to be taken prisoner, or even to suffer death, I dare say, had it been the alternative, had I been allowed to sleep. Indeed, some of the men could not resist its effects, and stepping aside off the road, threw themselves down, and yielded to its influence, although certain of being taken by the enemy, which they accordingly were.

Next day we halted in a meadow, where, having our rations served out, we proceeded on to a village, near which our light division and cavalry had a severe skirmish with the French, whom they repulsed. The enemy then retreated to their old position, and we were quartered in a Portuguese village, on the frontiers, within a few leagues of Roderigo, where we remained until January, 1812.

This was a miserable dirty place, with a few poor wretched inhabitants in it. It was designated by the soldiers, the "Hungry Village;" as, to answer some purpose which we were then unacquainted with, we had only half rations during the greater part of the time we were in it; to add to the rest, the officer in temporary command of the regiment at that time, was ignorant of his duty, which, in conjunction with a naturally cruel and vindictive disposition, bade fair to ruin the regiment in the few months he had the command of it. I shall not trace his pedigree to the low origin from whence he sprung, because, had he been a good man, it would only have enhanced his merit; nor shall I particularize the deformity of his person, which he could not help; but there will be no harm in giving a specimen of his mode of discipline while in command of the regiment, particularly as it forms a strong contrast to that of an officer whom I shall have occasion to mention in the course of this narrative.

Having neither the education nor the breeding of a gentleman, he felt jealous in the company of the officers, and lived in a retired and sullen manner. He generally passed his time in gossiping with his barber or his cook, or indeed any of the men, with an affectation of entering into all their concerns. By this and eavesdropping he became acquainted with little circumstances which another commanding officer would have disdained to listen to, and which he always made a bad use of. The full extent of his malevolent disposition was not known, however, until he got command of the regiment, when he introduced flogging for every trivial offence—in fact, the triangles were generally the accompaniment of every evening parade.

In addition to this, he invented more disgraceful and torturing modes of inflicting the punishment; but all this was not enough—he ordered that defaulters should have a patch of yellow and black cloth sewed on the sleeve of the regimental jacket, and a hole cut in it for every time they were flogged. The effects of this soon became visible: as good men were liable to be punished for the slightest fault, the barrier between them and hardened ill-doers was broken down, and as they had lost respect in their own eyes, they either became broken-hearted and inefficient soldiers, or grew reckless of everything, and launched into crime; those who were hardened and unprincipled before, being brought by the prevalence of punishment nearer a level with better men, seemed to glory in misconduct. In fact, all ideas of honour and character were lost, and listless apathy and bad conduct were the prevailing features of the corps at this time.

That flogging is notoriously useless in reclaiming men where they are bad, must be evident to everyone who knows anything of the service; and surely it is not politic to disgrace an individual, and break his heart for a casual error. There ought always to be an opening left for a man to retrieve a false step; but once bare his back at the halberts, and you shut it forever.

In the regiment I belonged to, I had a good opportunity of marking its effects, and in every instance, I have observed that it changed the individual's character for the worse; he either became broken-hearted and useless to the corps, or shameless and hardened. In two individual cases, its inefficiency to prevent the recurrence of the fault was particularly marked—the first was

142

desertion, and the second drunkenness. These men had received at various times upwards of two thousand lashes; but the first continued to absent himself, and the other to get drunk, periodically, although they were perfectly sure that flogging would be the result. There were men in the service to whom the excitement produced by ardent spirits seemed as necessary as food; in them this unnatural craving for liquor appeared to me to be a disease, calling for medical treatment more than punishment.

I have no doubt that many commanding officers resorted to corporal punishment from the conviction that it could not be done without; they had tried to dispense with it and could not—but I doubt much whether the experiment was fairly made. They found difficulties at the outset, and that it was more easy to exert their authority than their patience; the consequence was, that flogging was again resorted to, and they satisfied their conscience by saying that it could not be dispensed with. The real method of accomplishing the desired end was neglected, namely, making themselves acquainted with the character and disposition of the men under their command: this, I believe, many would think incompatible with their dignity; but has not a commanding officer as good a right to make himself acquainted with the dispositions of his men, as the medical officer with their constitutions? If they did so, they would soon find other means than flogging to make those under their command what they would wish them to be. I am aware that its frequency at one time had the effect of blinding the judgment of officers who possessed both feeling and discrimination; and I have occasionally witnessed a ludicrous waste of sympathy on some inferior animal, where nothing of the kind was felt for their fellow-creature suffering under the lash. For instance, I have known an officer shed tears when his favourite horse broke its leg, and next day exult in seeing a poor wretch severely flogged for being late of delivering an order; but I am happy to say, that the severe discipline of the old school is fast falling into disrepute, and I hope the time is not far distant when it will altogether be abolished.

The lieutenant-colonel joined when Captain L—— had

been some time exercising his power in this despotic manner; and being a man of a different stamp, he was not well pleased to find the men of his regiment, whom he had always been proud of, treated in this manner. His first order was to cut off all the badges which Captain L had ordered on the men. The frequent punishment was next done away, and the regiment was again placed on a fair footing; but the effect of their previous ill-usage did not so soon disappear.

This village was situated at the foot of a high hill, which was covered with wood, and from which the wolves were in the habit of coming down at night, and prowling about the village in quest of prey. On one post beside the field where the cattle were killed, the sentries were very much annoyed by them; but I believe they did no farther injury than devouring some pigs and an ass, which had been left out all night. Towards the end of December we were once or twice marched from our village, to within a short distance of Roderigo, for the purpose of intercepting supplies which the French attempted to throw into it, and the weather being extremely cold, we suffered much on the journey. The governor of that garrison (General Renaud) while out on a reconnoitring party about this time, was taken prisoner by the Spanish guerrilla chief, Don Julian.

In the beginning of January, 1812, we were removed for the purpose of besieging Ciudade Roderigo; and we left this miserable village in the midst of a snowstorm, and marched to Morti Agua. Next day we forded the Agueda, and took up our quarters in Ceridillo del Arroyo. The siege now commenced; the light division having succeeded, on the night of the 8th January, in storming one of the principal outworks, (the redoubt of St. Francisco,) we opened the trenches the same night, within six hundred yards of the town, the outwork which they had carried forming part of the first parallel.

The weather was so severe, and the cold so intense, that the army could not encamp, but the divisions employed at the siege marched from their different quarters and relieved each other alternately, every four-and-twenty hours. Our division took its turn of the duty on the 11th, and the frost was so excessive that we were almost completely benumbed, and nothing but hard working, I believe, kept us from perishing with the cold; indeed, it was said that some Portuguese soldiers actually died from its effects. Still, however, the work went on rapidly, and on the night of the 13th, another outwork (the fortified convent of Santa Cruz), was stormed by the 1st division, under General Graham.

On the 14th, the batteries in the first parallel were formed, and commenced firing from twenty-two pieces of cannon; that same night the 4th division carried all the remaining outworks, and we were established in the second parallel, one hundred and fifty yards from the town, on the 15th, on which day it fell our turn a second time for the duty.

The French kept up a very destructive fire on us during the whole of our operations, and while forming the second parallel they threw out some fire-balls to enable them to see where we were working, that they might send their shot in that direction; one of them fell very near where a party were working, and by its light completely exposed them to the view of the enemy; a sergeant belonging to our regiment, of the name of Frazer, seeing the danger to which they were exposed, seized a spade, and jumping out of the trench, regardless of the enemy's fire, ran forward to where it was burning, and having dug a hole, tumbled it in and covered it with earth.

On the morning of the 18th, a battery of seven guns was opened in the second parallel, while those in the first still continued their fire upon the walls. On the 19th our division again took their turn of the duty; but as the breaches were now considered practicable, the other troops destined for the attack were also assembled, it being Lord Wellington's intention to storm it that night.

The attack was directed to be made in five different columns: the two right, composed of part of our division, under the command of Major Ridge of the 5th regiment, and Colonel O'Toole of the 2nd Cacadores, were to protect the attack of the third column (composed of our right, brigade, commanded by General McKinnon) upon the principal breach; the left of this assault, was to be covered by part of the light division, who were, at the same time, to ascend the breaches on the left; while General Pack's brigade made a false attack on the south of the fort. On the right of the whole, the regiment I belonged to were to descend into the ditch, for the purpose of protecting the descent of General McKinnon's brigade against any obstacles which might be thrown in the way by the enemy.

Thus arranged, some time after it was dark, we moved down from our encampment towards the town, and our regiment having formed behind the walls of an old convent, each section being provided with a pickaxe and rope, we advanced rank entire under a heavy fire from the garrison, to the brink of the trench, where planting the one end of the pickaxe firmly in the ground, we threw the noose of the rope over the other, and then descended by it into the ditch. After descending, we moved along towards the breach. Our orders were to remain there, and protect the right brigade; but our colonel finding no obstacles in the way, pushed up the breach, leading on his regiment to the attack; the 5th regiment, which also belonged to the covering party, joined us as we ascended, and together we succeeded in establishing ourselves on the ramparts, in spite of the obstinate resistance made by the French.

The other troops advancing at the same time, we were masters of the town in half an hour from the commencement of the attack; but the gallant General McKinnon was killed by the springing of a mine, just as we gained the ramparts. The last time he was seen alive was when addressing a young officer who had displayed much courage—"Come," said he, "you are a fine lad, you and I will go together."

The next moment the mine sprung. In the morning his body was got a short distance from the place, wounded and blackened by the explosion. He was much regretted, for he was an intelligent, brave, and enterprising officer. General Crawford, a brave and much-beloved officer, who commanded the light division, was also mortally wounded in the assault.

The French had behaved well during the siege, and made a tolerable resistance at the breaches the night of the storm; but they appeared either to be panic-struck, not expecting us to storm the town so soon, or the individual who commanded wanted ability, for the dispositions made for the defence were a mere nothing, in comparison to those at Badajos, when that town was taken some time after. In mounting the breach, we found great difficulty in ascending, from the loose earth slipping from under our feet at every step, and throwing us down; the enemy at the same time pouring their shot amongst us from above. After having gained possession of the ramparts, the enemy retreated into a square in the centre of the town, where they were pursued, and gave up their arms.

Among the prisoners taken, were eighteen deserters from our army, who were subsequently tried and shot. The town was partially plundered by those who had straggled from their regiments, but the different columns remained formed on the ramparts until daylight, when a party from each regiment were sent to bury the dead, and collect the wounded, and I was one of the number.

The first we found was Captain W——, a brave and good officer. He fell mortally wounded near the head of the breach, while cheering on his men to the assault. Among the wounded lay Lieutenant T——, whom we used to call Robinson Crusoe, from his wearing very large whiskers, and always carrying a goatskin haversack, in which he kept the greater part of his necessaries, including his pipe and tobacco, of which he was very fond. The other officers rather shunned his company, from his not being very exact in his dress, and eccentric in his habits; but he was well liked by the soldiers, being an excellent officer, and brave as a lion. In this respect he was worth a hundred dandies. A few moments before he received the wound, he dragged a minikin officer from a hiding-place, and brandishing his sword over him, threatened to cut him down if he did not advance. But the poor fellow did not go many paces farther himself, when he was brought down by a grapeshot; yet still he continued to cheer on, and encourage the men who were ascending.

On the ascent of the breach lay many dead, and among the rest my ill-fated friend Sandy, whom I have had already occasion to mention, as parting from his wife at Jersey. When I saw him stretched lifeless on the breach, that scene flashed full upon my memory, and I could not but remark how true his wife's forebodings had turned out.

By taking the town, we became masters of one hundred and fifty-three pieces of cannon, including the heavy train of the French army, and a great number of stores. The Governor (General Banier), seventy-eight officers, and one thousand seven hundred men, were taken prisoners.

Our division was marched out of the town in the morning, and returned to the village where we were quartered. On the way home we lost one of our men, and we never heard of him after. It was suspected that he either perished among the snow, which lay thick on the ground, or that he was murdered by some of the peasantry.

CHAPTER 15

Badajoz Taken

After remaining a few days in Ceridillo del Arroyo, we removed to Villa Mayor, where we remained until we received orders to march back our old route to Badajos, which we invested on the 17th of March. Our division again taking the left of the Guidiana, along with the 4th and light, while the right was occupied by a brigade of General Hamilton's division, we broke ground rather to the left of our old trenches, within about two hundred yards of Fort Picurini, a strong outwork.

On the 19th the enemy made a sortie from one of the gates, a little to the right of our trenches, with two thousand men; but they were almost immediately driven in, without effecting anything, having suffered severely.

On the 25th we opened six batteries with twenty-eight pieces of cannon; and having kept up a heavy fire on Fort Picurini during the day, for the purpose of destroying the defences, when it was dark, a detachment of five hundred men of our division, under the command of Major General Kempt, were ordered to storm it. They were formed in three parties, who attacked at different places at the same time; and they succeeded, after an obstinate resistance, in gaining possession of it.

Two hundred men garrisoned the place, out of which one hundred and sixty were killed, or drowned in the overflow of the river. The colonel commanding, three other officers, and eighty-six men, were taken prisoners. Seven cannon were found in the place, besides some stores. During the assault, the enemy made a sortie from the town, with a view either to recover the place, or cover the retreat of the soldiers who manned it: but they were driven in by a party of the detachment stationed to protect the attack. In this affair we lost a great number of officers and men, some of them after the place was taken, the enemy having bombarded the fort from the town, when they found we were in possession of it.

The second parallel was now opened within three hundred yards of the town, in which two batteries commenced firing on the 28th. During this time the weather was so bad, and the rains so heavy, that we were working in the trenches up to the knees in mud, and the river swelled to such a height, that the pontoon bridge, over which we crossed the Guidiana, was carried away. On the 29th another sortie was made by the enemy on the right; but they were repulsed by General Hamilton's division. On the 31st twenty-seven pieces of cannon were opened in the second parallel, on the walls of the town; and the firing was continued with great effect until the 4th, when another battery of six guns was opened. Practicable breaches were effected on the 5th, and we were turned out that night to storm the town; but the enemy having made formidable preparations for the defence, the attack was deferred until next night, during which time all the guns in the second parallel were brought to bear upon the breaches. This delay was productive of very serious feeling throughout the succeeding day, as we were warned at the time to be ready to storm the town the next night.

Various were the effects produced on different individuals. There was an unusual talking of relations, a recalling to mind of scenes forgotten; a flow of kindly feeling which softened down the rough soldier into something milder and more pleasing. Many letters were written during that day to absent friends, in a more affectionate style than usual; and many injunctions given and taken, about writing, in the event of the fall of either party, to their relations.

The nearer the time drew for the intended attack, the more each individual seemed to shrink within himself; yet still nothing of fear or doubt of our success was expressed—every feeling displayed was natural and manly. At length night came, and the appointed hour for turning out.

It was dark and gloomy; not a single star showed its head; the air was still, not a sound could be heard but the noise of the field cricket, and the croaking of frogs; every word of command was given in a whisper, and the strictest silence enjoined, which I believe was unnecessary; few felt inclined to speak. At last the order was given to advance, and with palpitating hearts we commenced our march—slow and silent, a dead-weight hanging on every mind; had we been brought hurriedly into action, it would have been different, but it is inconsistent with the nature of man not to feel as I have described, in such a situation. The previous warning—the dark and silent night—the known strength of the place—the imminent danger of the attack—all conspired to produce it. Yet this feeling was not the result of want of courage; for I never witnessed anything like the calm intrepidity displayed in the advance, after we came within range of the enemy's cannon.

Being apprised of our intentions, they threw out fire-balls in every direction, and from total darkness, they changed the approaches to the garrison into a state light as day; by this means they were enabled to see the direction of our columns, and they opened a fire of round and grape-shot which raked through them, killing and wounding whole sections.

A circumstance occurred at this time, which may be worthy of notice. A man who had been very remarkable for his testy disposition, and inveterate habit of swearing on all occasions, happened to hit his foot against a stone, and stumbled; this vexed him, and uttering an oath, he wished a shot would come and knock his brains out; he had scarcely finished these words, when a grape-shot struck him in the forehead, and literally fulfilled the rash wish.

We still advanced, silent as before, save the groaning of our wounded comrades, until we reached a sort of moat about fifty feet wide, formed by the inundation of the river; here we had to pass, rank entire, the passage being only capable of admitting one at a time. On this place the enemy had brought their guns to bear, and they kept up such a fire of grape and musketry on it, that it was a miracle any of us escaped. When we reached the other side we formed again, and advanced up the glacis, forcing our way through the palisades, and got down into the ditch. The ladders by which we had to escalade the castle were not yet brought up, and the men were huddled on one another in such a manner that we could not move; we were now ordered to fix our bayonets.

When we first entered the trench, we considered ourselves comparatively safe, thinking we were out of range of their shot, but we were soon convinced of our mistake, for they opened several guns from angles which commanded the trench, and poured in grape-shot upon us from each side, every shot of which took effect, and every volley of which was succeeded by the dying groans of those who fell. Our situation at this time was truly appalling. The attack had commenced at the breaches towards our left, and the cannon and musketry which played upon our troops from every quarter of the town attacked, kept up a continual roll of thunder, and their incessant flash one quivering sheet of lightning; to add to the awfulness of the scene, a mine was sprung at the breach, which carried up in its dreadful blaze the mangled limbs and bodies of many of our comrades.

When the ladders were placed, each eager to mount, crowded them in such a way that many of them broke, and the poor fellows who had nearly reached the top, were precipitated a height of thirty or forty feet, and impaled on the bayonets of their comrades below; other ladders were pushed aside by the enemy on the walls, and fell with a crash on those in the ditch; while more who got to the top without accident were shot on reaching the parapet, and tumbling headlong, brought down those beneath them. This continued for some time, until at length a few having made a landing good on the ramparts, at the expense of their lives enabled a greater number to follow.

When about a company had thus got collected together, we

formed and charged round the ramparts, bayoneting the French artillery at their guns. In the direction that the party I was with took, they had drawn out a howitzer loaded to the very muzzle, pointed it towards us, and a gunner had the match ready to fire, when he was brought down by one of our party; in this direction we charged until we reached the sally-port communicating with the town. In a short time the whole division were established in possession of the castle, but the contest at the breaches was still severe.

The light and 4th divisions had advanced from the trenches a short time after us, until they reached the covered way; their advanced guards descended without difficulty into the ditch, and advanced to the assault with the most determined bravery, but such was the nature of the obstacles prepared by the enemy at the head of the breach, and behind it, that they could not establish themselves within the place. Repeated attempts were made until after twelve at night, when Lord Wellington finding that success was not to be obtained, and that our division had succeeded in taking the castle, they were ordered back to the ground where they had assembled, leaving the breach covered with dead and wounded.

When the governor (Philipon) found the castle was taken, he retreated into Fort St. Christoval, and at daylight in the morning he surrendered with all the garrison; it had consisted of five thousand men, of which number twelve hundred were killed during the siege.

When the town surrendered, and the prisoners were secured, the gate leading into the town from the castle was opened, and we were allowed to enter the town for the purpose of plundering it. We were scarcely through the gate when every regiment of the division were promiscuously mixed, and a scene of confusion took place which baffles description: each ran in the direction that pleased himself, bursting up the doors and rummaging through the houses, wantonly breaking up the most valuable articles of furniture found in them.

Small bands formed, and when they came to a door which

offered resistance, half-a-dozen muskets were levelled at the lock, and it flew up; by this means many men were wounded, for having entered at another door, there was often a number in the house, when the door was thus blown open. The greater number first sought the spirit-stores, where having drank an inordinate quantity, they were prepared for every sort of mischief. At one large vault in the centre of the town, to which a flight of steps led, they had staved in the heads of the casks, and were running with their hat-caps full of it, and so much was spilt here, that some, it was said, were actually drowned in it. Farther on, a number of those who had visited the spirit-store were firing away their ammunition, striving to hit some bells in front of a convent.

The effects of the liquor now began to show itself, and some of the scenes which ensued are too dreadful and disgusting to relate; where two or three thousand armed men, many of them mad drunk, others depraved and unprincipled, were freed from all restraint, running up and down the town, the atrocities which took place may be readily imagined—but in justice to the army, I must say they were not general, and in most cases perpetrated by cold-blooded villains, who were backward enough in the attack. Many risked their lives in defending helpless females, and although it was rather a dangerous place for an officer to appear, I saw many of them running as much risk to prevent inhumanity, as they did the preceding night in storming the town.

I very soon sickened of the noise, folly, and wickedness around me, and made out of the town towards the breach. When I arrived at where the attack had been made by the Light and 4th divisions, what a contrast to the scene I had just left! Here all was comparatively silent, unless here and there a groan from the poor fellows who lay wounded, and who were unable to move. As I looked round, several voices assailed my ear begging for a drink of water: I went, and having tilled a large pitcher which I found, relieved their wants as far as I could.

When I observed the defences that had been here made, I

could not wonder at our troops not succeeding in the assault. The ascent of the breach near the top was covered with thick planks of wood firmly connected together, staked down, and stuck full of sword and bayonet blades, which were firmly fastened into the wood with the points up; round the breach a deep trench was cut in the ramparts, which was planted full of muskets with the bayonets fixed, standing up perpendicularly, and firmly fixed in the earth up to the locks. Exclusive of this they had shell and hand grenades ready loaded piled on the ramparts, which they lighted and threw down among the assailants.

Round this place death appeared in every form, the whole ascent was completely covered with the killed, and for many yards around the approach to the walls, every variety of expression in their countenance, from calm placidity to the greatest agony.

Anxious to see the place where we had so severe a struggle the preceding night, I bent my steps to the ditch where we had placed the ladders to escalade the castle. The sight here was enough to harrow up the soul, and which no description of mine could convey an idea of. Beneath one of the ladders, among others lay a corporal of the 45th regiment, who, when wounded, had fallen forward on his knees and hands, and the foot of the ladder had been, in the confusion, placed on his back. Whether the wound would have been mortal, I do not know, but the weight of the men ascending the ladder had facilitated his death, for the blood was forced out of his ears, mouth, and nose.

Returning to the camp, I passed the narrow path across the moat, where many lay dead with their bodies half in the water. When I reached the opposite side, I perceived a woman with a child at her breast, and leading another by the hand, hurrying about with a distracted air, from one dead body to another, eagerly examining each. She came to one whose appearance seemed to strike her, (he was a grenadier of the 83rd regiment,) she hesitated some moments, as if afraid to realize the suspicion which crossed her mind. At length, seemingly determined to ascertain the extent of her misery, releasing the child from her hand, she raised the dead soldier, (who had fallen on his face,) and looking on his pallid features, she gave a wild scream, and the lifeless body fell from her arms. Sinking on her knees, she cast her eyes to heaven, while she strained her infant to her bosom with a convulsive gasp; the blood had fled her face, nor did a muscle of it move; she seemed inanimate, and all her faculties were absorbed in grief.

The elder child looked up in her face for some time with anxiety; at last he said, "Mother, why don't you speak to me?—what ails you?—what makes you so pale?—O speak to me, mother, do speak to me!"

A doubt seemed to cross her mind—without noticing the child, she again raised the mangled corpse, looked narrowly at his face, and carefully inspected the mark of his accoutrements—but it was too true—it was her husband. Neither sigh, nor groan, nor tear escaped her; but sitting down, she raised the lifeless body, and placing his head on her knee, gazed on his face with feelings too deep for utterance.

The child now drew himself close to her side, and looking at the bleeding corpse which she sustained, in a piteous tone, inquired, "Is that my father? is he asleep? why doesn't he speak to you? I'll waken him for you"—and seizing his hand, he drew it towards him, but suddenly relapsing his hold, he cried, "O mother! his hand is cold—cold as ice."

Her attention had been drawn for some moments to the child: at length bursting out, she exclaimed, "Poor orphan! he sleeps, never to wake again—never, O never, will he speak to you or me!" The child did not seem to understand her, but he began to cry. She continued, "O my God! my heart will burst, my very brain burns—but I can't cry—Surely my heart is hard—I used to cry when he was displeased with me—and now I can't cry when he is dead! O my husband! my murdered husband!—Ay, murdered," said she, wiping the blood that flowed from a wound in his breast. "O my poor children!" drawing them to her bosom, "what will become of you?" Here she began to talk incoherently—"Will you not speak to me, William?—will you not speak to your dear Ellen? Last night you told me you were going on guard, and you would return in the morning, but you did not come—I thought you were deceiving me, and I came to look for you."

She now ceased to speak, and rocked backwards and forwards over the bleeding corpse; but her parched quivering lip, and wild fixed look, showed the agonized workings of her mind. I stood not an unmoved spectator of this scene, but I did not interrupt it. I considered her sorrow too deep and sacred for commonplace consolation.

A woman and two men of the same regiment who had been in search of her, now came up and spoke to her, but she took no notice of them. A party also who were burying the dead joined them, and they crowded round striving to console her. I then withdrew, and hastened on to the camp, my mind filled with melancholy reflections; for many days after I felt a weight on my mind, and even now I retain a vivid recollection of that affecting scene. But she was not a solitary sufferer: many a widow and orphan was made by the siege and storming of Badajos; our loss amounting in killed and wounded to about three thousand men.

The camp during that day and for some days after was like a masquerade, the men going about intoxicated, dressed in the various dresses they had found in the town; French and Spanish officers, priests, friars, and nuns, were promiscuously mixed, cutting as many antics as a mountebank. It was some days before the army could be brought round to its former state of discipline. Indeed the giving leave to plunder the town, was productive of nothing but bad consequences, and for the interests of humanity, and the army at large, I hope such license may never recur, should we be again unfortunately plunged in war.

CHAPTER 16

Salamanca

A few days after the town was taken, I took the fever and ague, with which I was so extremely ill, that when we marched, which we did immediately after, I was unable to keep up with my regiment, and was left, with four others, about five leagues from Castello Branco, in charge of a sergeant, who was to endeavour to bring us on; but being unable to proceed, he was obliged to put us into a house in the small village in which we were left. It was occupied by a poor widow, who had two children; there was only one apartment in the house, in which there was a loom; and having crept under it, I lay there for four days without bed or covering, with the exception of an old great coat, my necessaries, which I was unable to carry, having gone forward with the regiment.

The poor Portuguese widow had little to give except commiseration, and seemed to feel much for me in particular, as the others could move about a little. I have often heard her, when she thought I was asleep, soliloquizing on the grief it would give my parents, were they to know my situation; and in her orisons, which she was in the habit of repeating aloud, she did not neglect a petition for the *"povre rapaz Englese."*[1] She often brought me warm milk, and pressed me to take a little of it; I felt very grateful for her sympathy and kindness, but I was too sick to taste it.

As we were here without any means of support, the sergeant

---

1. Poor English Boy.

managed to press five asses to carry us to Castello Branco, where there was a general hospital forming; on one of these I was mounted, and supported by the man who drove it. I took leave of the tender-hearted widow, while the tears stood in her eyes. Such disinterested feeling I was at that time little accustomed to, and it was precious. We proceeded on our journey, but never did I endure such torture as I did on that day, and I often begged of them to allow me to lie down and die.

On the second day we reached our destination, and remained waiting in the street for two hours before the general doctor would look at us. When he did come, his countenance foreboded no good.

"What's the matter with you, sir?" said he to me, in a scowling tone of voice; "You ought to have been with your regiment; a parcel of lazy skulking fellows—there's nothing the matter with any of you!"

I said nothing, but I looked in his face, with a look which asked him if he really believed what he said, or if he did not read a different story in my pale face and sunken cheek. He seemed to feel the appeal, and softening his countenance he passed on to another. We were then placed along with others, in the passage of a convent, which was converted into an hospital; here I lay that day on the floor, without mattress or covering.

Night came, and a burning fever raged through my veins; I called for drink, but there was no one to give it me. In the course of the night I became delirious; the last thing I remember was strange fantastic shapes flitting around me, which now and then catched me up, and flew with me like lightning through every obstacle—then they would hold me over a precipice, and letting me fall, I would continue sinking, with a horrid consciousness of my situation, until my mind was lost in some wild vagary of a different nature. For some days I was unconscious of what was passing, and when I recovered my senses, I found myself in a small apartment with others who had bad fevers, but I was now provided with a mattress and bed-clothes.

A poor fellow, a musician of the 43rd regiment, was next

berth to me, sitting up in his bed in a fit of delirium, addressing himself to some young females, whom he supposed to be spinning under the superintendence of an old woman, in a corner of the ceiling; he kept a constant conversation with his supposed neighbours, whom he seemed to think were much in awe of the old dame, and he frequently rose out of his bed to throw up his handkerchief as a signal. When he recovered, the impression was so strong, that he remembered every particular.

There was a great want of proper attendants in the hospital, and many a time I have heard the sick crying for drink and assistance during the whole night, without receiving it. There seemed also to be a scarcity of medical officers during the Peninsular war. I have known wounded men often to be three days after an engagement before it came to their turn to be dressed; and it may be safely calculated that one-half of those men were thus lost to the service. Those medical men we had were not always ornaments of the profession. They were chiefly, I believe, composed of apothecaries' boys, who, having studied a session or two, were thrust into the army as a huge dissecting-room, where they might mangle with impunity, until they were drilled into an ordinary knowledge of their business; and as they began at the wrong end, they generally did much mischief before that was attained. The extent of their medical practice in most disorders was to "blister, bleed, and purge,"—what then? Why "blister, bleed, and purge," again. This method of cure with poor wretches who were anything but overfed, and whose greatest complaint often was fatigue and want of proper sustenance, was quite *a-la*-Hornbook, and the sufferers were quickly laid to rest. In the field they did more mischief, being but partially acquainted with anatomy; there was enough of what medical men call *bold practice*. In cutting down upon a ball for the purpose of extracting it, ten chances to one but they severed an artery they knew not how to stem; but this gave no concern to these enterprising fellows, for clapping a piece of lint and a bandage, or a piece of adhesive plaster on the wound, they would walk off very composedly to mangle some other poor wretch, leaving the former to his fate.

Here I may be accused of speaking at random, on a subject I do not understand; but there is no man who served in the Peninsular war, but can bear witness to the truth of what I have stated. I, however, do not pretend to say there were not many exceptions to this character; and in justice to the whole, it must be admitted, that the duties of a surgeon on the Peninsula, were fatiguing and arduous in the extreme. The medical department of the French army was much superior to ours at that time in every respect; this can only be accounted for by the superior opportunity they had of studying anatomy, which in Britain is now almost prohibited—more the pity! Those who have witnessed the evils resulting to the army in particular, from imperfectly educated surgeons, must regret that government does not afford greater facilities to the study.

The ague fits having returned when the severe fever left me, I recovered very slowly; the medicine I received, which was given very irregularly, having done me no good. While in this state, General Sir John Hope, who lately commanded the forces in Scotland, happened to pay a visit to the hospital, and going round the sick with the staff-surgeon, he inquired "What was the prevailing disease?"

The reply was, "Fever and ague."

Sir John, whose kind and humane disposition is well known, mentioned that he had heard of a cure for that disease among the old women in Scotland, which was considered infallible. The staff-surgeon smiled, and begged to hear what it was.

"It is," said the good old general, "simply a large pill formed of spider's web, to be swallowed when the fit is coming on. I cannot pledge myself for its efficacy, but I have heard it much talked of."

The staff-doctor gave a shrug, as much as to say, it was all nonsense, looked very wise, as all doctors endeavour to do, and the conversation dropped.

I had been listening eagerly to the conversation, and no sooner was the general gone, than I set out in quest of the specific. I did not need to travel far, and returned to my room prepared for the next fit; when I felt it coming on, I swallowed the dose with the greatest confidence in its virtues, and however strange it may appear, or hard to be accounted for, I never had a fit of the ague after, but got well rapidly, and was soon fit to march for the purpose of joining my regiment, which I overtook at Pollos. They had been quartered for some weeks in a village on the frontiers, from whence they advanced, and having passed Salamanca, were now in this place, which was situated on a rising ground on the bank of the river Douro, our army occupying the one side, and the French the other.

In this place we were in the habit of turning out of the town during the night, and lying under arms in the field; in the day we occupied the village, still wearing our accoutrements. Fuel was uncommonly scarce; the inhabitants in the best of times, having only the prunings of their vines for that purpose, and we were obliged to cook our victuals with stubble. While here there was an understanding, I believe, between both armies, that each should have the use of the river without molestation, and our men and the French used to swim in it promiscuously, mixing together, and at times bringing brandy and wine with them, for the purpose of treating each other; but though thus friendly to our men, the French soldiers studiously avoided coming near the Portuguese, whom they knew by the dark colour of their skin.

This friendly feeling between our soldiers and the French was remarkably displayed during the whole war, whenever we were brought in position close to each other, or either party were taken prisoners; and it could only be accounted for by the respect excited by the bravery of each nation, and a similar generosity of sentiment, for in this the French were not deficient. How different were our feelings in this respect from many of our countrymen at home, whose ideas of the French character were drawn from servile newspapers and pamphlets, or even from so low a source as the caricatures in print-shops; but I myself must confess, in common with many others, that I was astonished when I came in contact with French soldiers, to find them, instead of pigmy, spider-shanked wretches, who fed on nothing but frogs and beef tea, stout, handsome-looking fellows, who understood the principles of good living, as well as any Englishman amongst us; and whatever may be said to the contrary, remarkably brave soldiers.

During the time we lay in this position, a German, belonging to our band deserted to the enemy, taking with him a horse and two mules; he had taken them down to the river to drink, and led them through to the opposite side, in the face of both armies; when he reached the opposite bank, the French lifted him on their shoulders, and leading the cattle behind him, carried him up to their camp in triumph, cheering all the way.

From this place, in consequence of orders to that effect, we retired upon Salamanca, followed by the enemy, and took up our position about a mile and a half from that town, on the right bank of the river Tormes, where we lay until the 22nd of July. On the evening of the 21st it came on a dreadful storm of thunder and lightning, which so terrified the horses and mules, who were fastened to stakes in the camp, that they broke loose and ran about in every direction, causing great confusion.

On the morning of the 22nd, having recrossed the Tormes, we took up our position in front of Salamanca, behind the village of Aldea Teja. The enemy, who had manoeuvred during the forenoon, about two o'clock began to extend their left, and moved forward on our position, which was now taken up—the seventh division on the right, the fourth and fifth in the centre, while the first and light divisions on our left were opposed to the enemy's right, and were, with the fifth division, in reserve.

The attack commenced by our division, in four columns, moving forward, supported by a body of cavalry, to turn the enemy's left; we were led on by General Packenham, (General Picton having gone to the rear sick a few days before,) and completely succeeded; for having formed across the enemy's flank, we advanced under a heavy fire from their artillery, overthrowing everything before us. The fifth regiment, in attacking a body of infantry posted on a small height, were furiously charged by the enemy's cavalry, and thrown into some confusion: but ours coming up in time, not only routed them, but cut off the retreat of their infantry, who were taken prisoners, many of them dreadfully wounded by our dragoons, some having their arms hanging by a shred of flesh and skin, and others with hideous gashes in their faces.

In this manner driving in their left, we came in front of where our artillery were playing on the enemy; but no time was lost, for by marching past in open column, they continued to fire without interruption, sending their shot through the intervals between each company, without doing us any injury, although it created rather unpleasant sensations to hear it whistling past us. The enemy's shot and shell were now making dreadful havoc. A Portuguese cadet who was attached to our regiment, received a shell in the centre of his body, which, bursting at the same instant, literally blew him to pieces. Another poor fellow receiving a grape shot across his belly, his bowels protruded, and he was obliged to apply both his hands to the wound to keep them in; I shall never forget the expression of agony depicted in his countenance. These were remarkable cases, but the men were now falling thick on every side.

During the time we were thus successfully engaged, the fourth and fifth divisions advanced on the enemy's centre, supported by Sir Stapleton Cotton's cavalry, and drove them from one position after another with great slaughter; but they were in some measure retarded in their progress by a fresh body of troops being pushed forward on their left, from a height which the enemy had continued to hold in spite of the efforts of a brigade of our troops under General Pack. This accession of force was so powerful, that the fourth division was now brought up, and success was restored; but the enemy's right, which was reinforced by those who had fled from the left, and who had occupied the heights above-mentioned, still made a stand; the first and light divisions now had their turn of the battle, and attacking them with determined vigour, in a short time succeeded in turning their right. The flanks being now turned, the centre was attacked by the sixth division, supported by ours and the fourth; but the enemy made a brave and most determined resistance, and it was dark before the point was carried.

The French then broke up in great confusion, and fled through the woods towards the fords of the Tormes, pursued by the cavalry and first and light divisions, as long as any of them could be found together. Next morning the pursuit was renewed at daybreak by the same troops, who, having crossed the Tormes, came up with the enemy's rear-guard of cavalry and infantry; they were immediately attacked by our dragoons, and the French cavalry fled, leaving the infantry unprotected, who were charged by the heavy cavalry of our German legion, and the whole body, consisting of three battalions, were taken prisoners.

During the battle, the Spanish army, under Don Carlos d'Espagne, had remained at a respectable distance on a height in our rear without having been engaged; they seemed to be perfectly contented with seeing us fighting for their country, without having a hand in it themselves; and when we were successful, they threw up their caps in the air, and cheered as heartily as if they had earned the victory; they had only one or two men wounded of their whole army, while ours lost nearly the half of its number in killed and wounded.

In this engagement twenty pieces of cannon were taken, several ammunition wagons, two eagles, and six colours; one general, three colonels, three lieutenant, colonels, one hundred and thirty officers of inferior rank, and between six and seven thousand prisoners. Four generals were killed and General Marmont severely wounded.

The French continuing their retreat, our army, passing Alba de Tormes and Penaranda, continued their advance towards Madrid, some leagues from which, there was a severe skirmish between the French cavalry and some of our German dragoons. The Portuguese cavalry had been first engaged, but behaving ill, the Germans were obliged to take their place, and soon retrieved the day. When we passed the village where the skirmish had taken place, those who had fallen were lying on the roadside, and our attention was drawn particularly to one of the French cavalry, who had received such a dreadful blow, that his head was completely cleft through his brass helmet.

Passing on, we encamped about half a league from Madrid on the 11th of August, and in a short time our camp was filled with the inhabitants who had come out to see us, and in their own language, welcomed us as their deliverers. On the 12th, being ordered to march into the town, we were met by the inhabitants carrying branches of laurel, and playing on guitars and tambourines; joy beamed on every countenance, the ladies thronged round the British colours eager to touch them, and the air was rent with acclamations—"*Viva los Engleses,*" echoed from every mouth. The windows were hung with embroidered cloth, and filled with ladies waving their handkerchiefs.

This was a proud day for the British army. Having marched up to the Placa del Sol, we took up our quarters in a large building; but our work was not yet finished.

The French having fortified the Retiro, had left a garrison in it, whose outposts were established in the Prado and botanic garden; but that night a detachment having driven them in, broke through the wall in several places, and established themselves in the palace of Retiro, close to the exterior of the enemy's works, enclosing the building called La China. Next morning, the 13th, we were turned out and assembled on the Prado, with scaling ladders ready to attack the works, when they capitulated, and were allowed to march out with the honours of war, the officers their baggage, and soldiers their knapsacks, and surrendered themselves prisoners.

There was found in the garrison one hundred and eighty-nine pieces of brass cannon, nine hundred barrels of gunpowder, twenty-thousand stand of arms, and considerable magazines of clothing, provisions, and, ammunition, with the eagles of the 13th and 51st regiments. Having relieved their guards, they marched out at four o'clock in the afternoon, two thousand five hundred and six men, among whom were two colonels, four lieutenant-colonels, twenty-two captains, and thirty-five subalterns.

We were now peaceably quartered in the town, having time to look about us and recover from our former fatigues. No place could have been better adapted for this than Madrid; the air was pure and healthy; wine, fruit, and provision, good and cheap. Here we had food for observation in the buildings, institutions, and manners of the inhabitants, and we ranged about in the environs, and from one street to another, as if we had been in a new world. Madrid has been so often described by writers of ability, that it would be presumption in me to attempt it, even did the limits of this work allow; but the delightful walks of the Prado, the gardens breathing perfume—the beautiful fountains—the extensive and picturesque view from the Segovia gate—the cool and delicious shades on the banks of the Manzanares—their women—their music and nightly serenades, gave it to my mind the charm of romance.

During the time we remained in Madrid, our troops were allowed free access to the museum, in the street Alcala, nearly opposite our barracks. In it there was a very valuable collection of natural history, particularly a lump of native gold brought from South America, which weighed many pounds, some enormous boa constrictors, and the entire skeleton of a mammoth. This, like the British Museum, was free to all visitors three or four days a week.

Several times daring our stay in Madrid we were admitted, *gratis*, to see the bullfights, the great national amusement of the Spaniards. The place of these exhibitions was a vast amphitheatre, with three tiers of boxes ranged along the wall, the roof of the building projecting so far over as to cover them only, all the rest being open. In the highest range of these on the shade side, was the king's box, gorgeously decorated, those on its right and left being occupied by the principal nobility. About a dozen seats sloping from the lowest tier of boxes formed the pit, where the common people were admitted, and which varied in the price of admission, according to the degree of shade afforded. In front of the pit was a passage of a few feet wide, separated from the arena by a barricade between five and six feet high. The arena or space where the bulls were fought was of great dimensions; two main passages opened into it through the barricade, one by which the bulls were drawn off when killed, and the other by which they entered, communicating with a place where they were kept previous to the fight, that resembled, in some degree, a large cage, having spaces between the planks that covered it, where they goaded and otherwise tormented the animals, to render them more savage before they entered the arena. But besides these entrances there were smaller doors opening into the passage, by which the bull could be driven back into the area, in the event of his leaping the barricade, this being no infrequent occurrence.

I only witnessed the sight once. Lord Wellington was present, and sat in a box on the right of the king's, the royal box being empty. The performance commenced by a guard of soldiers marching into the centre of the arena, forming a circle, and on a signal by beat of drum, facing outwards, and marching up to the barricade, where, placing a foot on a step, on the next signal, they vaulted over in the passage, where they stood during the exhibition.

The horseman who was to attack the bull, now entered, dressed somewhat in the same manner as our equestrians or rope-dancers, armed with a spear, rolled round with cord to within half an inch of the point, to prevent the wound which he might give the animal from proving mortal. With him also entered the men on foot, whose office was to irritate or divert the attention of the bull from the horseman when in too great danger. They were dressed in nearly the same style, only carrying different-coloured mantles or cloaks.

The signal was now given for the performance to commence. The footmen ranged themselves round the barricade, while the horseman, placing his spear in the rest, remained opposite to, and some distance from, the door by which the bull was to enter. All being thus prepared, the door was thrown open—the animal rushed furiously out, his nostrils dilated, and his eyeballs gleaming fire. A flight of pigeons which were let off at his head as he entered the arena, irritated him, and attracted his attention a little; but perceiving the horseman, he began to roar and paw the ground, and rushed forward upon him. The horse being urged to a gallop, he was met halfway, and struck by the spear on the shoulder, and fairly thrown on his hind legs, bellowing fearfully with the pain of the wound. The horse had now started aside, and when the animal regained his feet, which he did almost instantaneously, he was surrounded by the footmen, who, whenever he made a charge at one of them, threw a mantle over his head, and while he tossed it, and roared to get rid of it, danced round, planting arrows in his sides and neck filled with crackers, which, by the time he got free of the cloak, began to go off, and maddened him to the utmost degree. His appearance at this time was terrific.

The horseman was now prepared for a second charge, which being made, the bull was again attacked by the footmen, who often ran imminent danger, being pushed so closely that they were obliged to leap the barricade. This alternate attack was continued several times, until the people being tired, the matador was called for, who entered on foot without any defence but a small sword.

The men on foot still continued to irritate the animal, until it was roused to the utmost pitch of madness, when the matador placing himself in its way, in the midst of one of its most furious attacks, calmly waited its approach. Seeing the bull close upon him, we expected that the man would be gored to death—that there was no possibility of his escape. But the moment the enraged animal came within his reach, he darted the sword, quick as lightning, between the horns into the back of his neck, and he fell dead at his feet without giving a single struggle. The music now began to play, and amidst the deafening plaudits of the spectators, six mules gaily caparisoned entered, and having their traces fastened to the dead bull, dragged him from the arena.

Six bulls were thus despatched without much variation in the mode; but one of them, (of Andalusian breed,) remarkable for its strength and fierceness, having been missed by the horseman in his attempt to strike him, came on so furiously that he had not time to escape, and the bull running the poor horse up against the barricade, lowered his head, and bringing up his horns, tore up his belly in such a way, that part of his bowels protruded at the wound, and hung down to the ground. The horseman, who had with great agility drawn up his leg, was now supported from falling by those who were in the passage, his right leg being jammed in between the horse and the barricade. The attention of the animal was soon drawn off by the men on foot; and the man was no sooner released from his dangerous situation, than, mounting afresh the wounded animal, he endeavoured to push it forward to another charge, with its bowels trailing on the ground. This action, which deserved to be execrated as a piece of wanton cruelty, was lauded to the skies, and cries of *"Bravo! bravo!"* resounded from every quarter. But the poor animal only moved a few steps, when it fell down dead.

The bull was now enraged so much that nothing could divert him from his purpose, and having followed one of the footmen to the limits of the arena, fairly leaped the barricade after him. A scene of dreadful confusion ensued, those in the pit and passage flying in every direction. The danger was soon over, however, for opening one of the doors already mentioned, he was driven back into the arena, and despatched by the matador.

The last bull ushered in was baited by dogs. I do not believe that many of our men were much captivated with this amusement; it was rather considered a cruel and disgusting one. I cannot understand how it is so much encouraged in Spain, unless it be to serve the same purpose that we pay boxers to murder each other, namely, to keep up the national courage.

I have known some of those "bruising" fellows in the army—indeed every regiment has its "bully;" but although they were always forward enough to abuse and tyrannize over their fellow-soldiers, who were not of the "fancy," I never knew one of them that displayed even ordinary courage in the field; and it was invariably by fellows of this description that outrages, such as those perpetrated at Badajos, were committed.

While in Madrid, one of their state prisoners was executed for treason: I do not remember his rank or name, but the mode of execution was so singular, that it may be worth describing.

On the day appointed for his execution, a scaffold was raised in the Placa Real, or Royal Square. In the centre of this platform there was fixed an apparatus, resembling a chair, only, in place of the usual back, there was an upright stake; to this there was fastened an iron collar, which by means of a screw behind, could be tightened or relaxed at pleasure. A vast concourse of people had assembled to see the criminal suffer. He was led to the place of execution on an ass, having his arms pinioned, a crucifix in his hand, and surrounded by priests. On mounting the scaffold, he was placed on the seat already described, bound firmly down, and the priest took his place in front of him, with a crucifix in his hand, and from his violent gesticulations, seemed to be exhorting him very earnestly. This ceremony finished, the garrotte or collar was placed about his neck, and his face covered. The executioner stood prepared, and on the signal being given, as far as I recollect, one wrench did the business, having completely flattened his neck. In this situation he remained a considerable time, when the body was removed, and the crowd dispersed.

CHAPTER 17

Retreat to Portugal

About the 24th of October, we marched from Madrid to Pinto, a distance of about three leagues; in consequence of the enemy advancing in great force, in that direction. Here we remained until the 30th, when we were ordered to retreat upon Madrid, and passed our pontoons burning on the roadside, having been set on fire to prevent them falling into the hands of the enemy.

We supposed at first that we would again occupy Madrid, but when we came in sight of it the Retiro was in flames, and we could hear the report of cannon, which proceeded from the brass guns in the fort being turned on each other for the purpose of rendering them useless to the enemy; the stores of provision and clothing which we had previously taken were also burned, and every preparation made for evacuating the place. The staff officers were galloping about giving directions to the different divisions concerning their route; the inhabitants whom we met on the road were in evident consternation, and everything indicated an unexpected and hurried retreat: instead, therefore, of entering the city, we passed to the left of it. The enemy's cavalry by this time being close on our rear, and before ours had evacuated the town on the one side, the French had entered it on the other. We marched about a league past Madrid, when we encamped for the night; but next morning we proceeded on our retreat, nor halted until we reached Salamanca, having the enemy encamped close on our rear every night.

The French having taken up nearly the same position they had occupied on the 22nd of July, on the afternoon of the 15th November we turned out of the town, and forming on nearly our old ground, expected an immediate engagement. We had been so much harassed in retreating from Madrid in the severe weather, that we felt much more inclination to fight than to go farther, but we were disappointed; and after performing some evolutions, we filed off on the road leading to Roderigo, and commenced retreating as night was setting in. I never saw the troops in such a bad humour.

Retreating before the enemy at any time was a grievous business, but in such weather it was doubly so; the rain, now pouring down in torrents, drenched us to the skin, and the road, composed of a clay soil, stuck to our shoes so fast, that they were torn off our feet. The night was dismally dark, the cold wind blew in heavy gusts, and the roads became gradually worse. After marching in this state for several hours, we halted in a field on the road side, and having piled our arms, were allowed to dispose ourselves to rest as we best could.

The moon was now up, and wading through the dense masses of clouds, she sometimes threw a momentary gleam on the miserable beings who were huddled together in every variety of posture, endeavouring to rest or screen themselves from the cold. Some were lying stretched on the wet ground rolled in still wetter blankets, more having placed their knapsack on a stone, or their wooden canteen, had seated themselves on it with their blankets wrapped about them, their head reclining on their knees, and their teeth chattering with cold; while others more resolute and wise, were walking briskly about. Few words were spoken, and as if ashamed to complain of the hardships we suffered, execrating the retreat, and blaming Lord Wellington for not having sufficient confidence in us to hazard a battle with the enemy, under any circumstances, were the only topics discussed.

A considerable time before daylight we were again ordered to fall in, and proceeded on our retreat. The rain still continued to fall, and the roads were knee deep. Many men got fatigued and unable to proceed. Some spring-wagons were kept in the rear to bring them up, but the number increased so fast that there was soon no conveyance for them; and as we formed the rearguard, they soon fell into the hands of the French cavalry, who hung on our rear during the whole retreat.

When we came to our halting ground, the same accommodation awaited us as on the preceding evening. By some mismanagement the commissary stores had been sent on with the rest of the baggage to Roderigo, and we were without food. The feeling of hunger was very severe. Some beef that had remained with the division was served out to us, but our attempts to kindle fires with wet wood were quite abortive. Sometimes, indeed, we managed to raise a smoke, and numbers gathered round, in the vain hope of getting themselves warmed, but the fire would extinguish in spite of all their efforts. Our situation was truly distressing: tormented by hunger, wet to the skin, and fatigued in the extreme, our reflections were bitter; the comfortable homes and firesides which we had left were now recalled to mind, and contrasted with our present miserable situation; and during that night many a tear of repentance and regret fell from eyes "unused to the melting mood."

About the same hour as on the preceding morning, we again fell in and marched off, but the effects of hunger and fatigue were now more visible. A savage sort of desperation had taken possession of our minds, and those who had lived on the most friendly terms in happier times, now quarrelled with each other, using the most frightful imprecations on the slightest offence. All former feeling of friendship was stifled, and a misanthropic spirit took possession of every bosom. The streams which fell from the hills were swelled into rivers, which we had to wade, and vast numbers fell out, among whom were officers, who, having been subject to the same privation, were reduced to the most abject misery.

It was piteous to see some of the men, who had dragged their limbs after them with determined spirit until their strength failed, fall down amongst the mud, unable to proceed farther; and as they were sure of being taken prisoners, if they escaped being trampled to death by the enemy's cavalry, the despairing farewell look that the poor fellows gave us when they saw us pass on, would have pierced our hearts at any other time; but our feelings were steeled, and so helpless had we become, that we had no power to assist, even had we felt the inclination to do so.

Among the rest, one instance was so distressing, that no one could behold it unmoved. The wife of a young man, who had endeavoured to be present with her husband on every occasion, if possible, having kept up with us amidst all our sufferings from Salamanca, was at length so overcome by fatigue and want, that she could go no farther. For some distance, with the assistance of her husband's arm, she had managed to drag her weary limbs along, but at length she became so exhausted, that she stood still, unable to move. Her husband was allowed to fall out with her, for the purpose of getting her into one of the spring-wagons, but when they came up, they were already loaded in such a manner that she could not be admitted, and numbers in the same predicament were left, lying on the roadside. The poor fellow was now in a dreadful dilemma, being necessitated either to leave her to the mercy of the French soldiers, or by remaining with her to be taken prisoner, and even then perhaps be unable to protect her.

The alternative either way was heartrending; but there was no time to lose—the French cavalry were close upon them. In despairing accents she begged him not to leave her, and at one time he had taken the resolution to remain; but the fear of being considered as a deserter urged him to proceed, and with feelings easier imagined than described, he left her to her fate, and never saw her again; but many a time afterwards did he deprecate his conduct on that occasion, and the recollection of it embittered his life.

On this night the rain had somewhat abated, but the cold was excessive, and numbers who had resisted the effects of the hunger and fatigue with a hardy spirit, were now obliged to give way to its overpowering influence, and sunk to the ground praying for death to relieve them from their misery; and some prayed not in vain, for next morning before daylight, in passing from our halting ground to the road, we stumbled over several who had died during the night. Inadvertently I set my foot on one of them, and stooped down to ascertain whether the individual was really dead, and I shall never forget the sickening thrill that went to my heart, when my hand came in contact with his cold and clammy face. On this day our hearts seemed to have wholly failed us: to speak was a burden, and the most helpless weakness pervaded every individual; we had now arrived at that pitch of misery which levels all distinction of rank, and I believe no order would have been obeyed unless that which was prompted by regard to the common safety.

Dennis, round whom there used to be gathered a host of his comrades, listening to his witticisms or quaint remarks, and whose spirits I had never known to fail, was now crestfallen, and moved along with the greatest difficulty. Nothing but death, however, could altogether keep down his buoyant spirits; for if we got a minute's halt during the march, he made such ludicrous remarks on the woebegone countenances of himself or his companions, that, although the effort was distressing, they were obliged to smile in spite of their misery.

This day we halted sooner than usual, and the weather being clearer, we got fires kindled—still no rations; but we were encamped among oak-trees, and greedily devoured the acorns which grew upon them, although nauseous in the extreme, the officer commanding the brigade and our colonel joining in the repast. In many respects the officers were in a worse situation than the men, not having anything to change themselves, as their baggage had been sent on before us.

If anything could have given us comfort in our miserable situation, it was having a kind and sympathizing commanding officer: he made many of the weakly men throw away their knapsacks, and by every means in his power he endeavoured to infuse comfort and courage into their sinking hearts, braving every difficulty in common with the meanest individual, and even rejected the superior accommodation which his rank afforded, while he saw the men suffering. It was in a situation like this where true greatness of mind could be displayed; and there must have been something innately great and noble in the mind which could thus rise superior even to nature. In my opinion, a much greater degree of real courage was necessary to brave the horrors of this retreat, than to face the fire of a battery.

During the night our situation was worse than in the day, for there was then nothing to divert our attention from our wretched state; and although we despaired of ever seeing it, we felt that indescribable longing after home, which everyone must have felt in the same situation. It will be needless to detail our next day's sufferings—they were of the same nature as the preceding, only more aggravated.

We were now drawing near Roderigo, where our baggage had been ordered; each day our hopes had been kept alive in the expectation that we would find provision at our halting-place, but we were deceived. Now, however, these expectations were more likely to be realized.

About dusk we took up our ground on the face of a hill near Roderigo, and the weather changing to a severe frost, was intensely cold. We had not been long halted when the well-known summons of "Turn out for biscuit," rang in our ears. The whole camp was soon in a bustle, and some of the strongest having gone for it, they received two days' rations for each man. It was customary to divide it, but on this night it was dispensed with, and each eagerly seizing on what he could get, endeavoured to allay the dreadful gnawing which had tormented us during four days of unexampled cold and fatigue. In a short time, two rations more were delivered, and the inordinate eating that ensued threatened to do more mischief than the former want.

We went into quarters next day, and many who had borne up during the retreat now fell sick, and were sent to the hospital.

From this place, we removed in a few days some way into Portugal, where we took up our winter quarters in a small village, called Fonte Arcada.

CHAPTER 18

Fonte Arcada

Fonte Arcada, in which our regiment was quartered (the remainder of the division being distributed in the surrounding villages), was situated on the face of a hill, which formed one of an extensive range; at its foot ran one of the tributary streams of the Douro, meandering through a fertile and tolerably well-cultivated valley.

The village itself was built on a bare and rugged mass of rock, and the frowning ledge that hung over the town gave it a wild and romantic air. The place had not escaped the ravages of war, but being more out of the common route, it had suffered little in comparison to others. The houses had rather a mean appearance, with the exception of three or four belonging to *fidalgos*, who resided in the village; but the situation was healthy. And after we had cleaned it (which we had to do with every Portuguese village before we could inhabit them), we felt ourselves very comfortable, and soon forgot all our former fatigue, which we did the readier, that we had now a commanding officer who interested himself warmly in our welfare.

Lieutenant-Colonel Lloyd had joined us from the 43d regiment. I have already had occasion to mention him, in describing the retreat from Salamanca. No eulogium, however, of mine can convey an idea of his merits as a man and soldier; but it is deeply engraven on the hearts of those who served under him.

So harmoniously did he blend the qualities of a brave, active, intelligent officer with those of the gentleman and the scholar, that the combination fascinated all ranks. His exterior corresponded with his mind: he was somewhat above the middle size—and to a face and head cast in the true Roman mould, was joined an elegant and manly body. His system of discipline was not coercive; he endeavoured to encourage, not to terrify—if there was a single spark of pride or honour in the bosom, he would fan it to a flame. His aim was to prevent crime rather than to punish it, and he rarely resorted to corporal punishment. When he did so, it was only in the case of hardened ill-doers, with whom no lenient measures would succeed; even then, he never punished to the tenth part of the sentence awarded; and if the culprit sued for pardon, promising not to be guilty again, he would say, "I take you at your word, and forgive you, but remember your promise."

The men's interests formed his chief study, and the complaint of the meanest individual was heard and investigated with the strictest impartiality, without respect to persons. By the measures he took, he made every individual interested in his own honour and that of the regiment; and I believe that every man in it loved and honoured him. So successful were his efforts, that he brought the regiment into a state of order, cleanliness, and discipline, which could never have been attained by any other means. He was always the first in danger and the last out of it; and in camp, he went later to rest, and was sooner up than the meanest individual composing his corps.

He was a native of Ireland (Limerick, I believe), and a striking corroboration of the general remark, that where an Irishman is a gentleman, he is one in the most extensive meaning of the word: unfettered by cold, calculating selfishness, his noble heart and soul is seen in everything he does—such was Colonel Lloyd.

The inhabitants here were similar to those we had met with in other villages in Portugal—sunk in ignorance, dirt, and superstition; and although some of the *fidalgos* boasted that the blood of Braganza flowed in their veins, they did not seem to be a whit more refined or better informed than the plebeians. They were rigid attendants on all the religious ceremonies of their church, but religion with them appeared to be a mere habit—it played on the surface, but did not reach the heart. When the bell rang at stated periods for prayers, each rosary was put in requisition; but this did not interrupt the conversation—they managed to pray and converse at the same time. As bigotry is always the attendant of ignorance, they were no way liberal in their opinions concerning us; and so contaminated did they consider us by heresy, that they would not drink out of the same vessel. But to tell the truth, I believe they did not understand the principles of the religion they professed, and the "Padre Cura" of the village (a gross and un-spiritual-looking piece of furniture) did not seem much qualified to inform them.

We remained here near six months, during which vigorous preparations were made for the ensuing campaign, but little occurred interesting or worth recording while quartered in the village, with the exception of a love affair in which my friend Henry was engaged, which is so tinged with romance that I could scarcely expect credence to the detail, were it not that all who were then present with the regiment can vouch for its truth.

Henry, whose warm heart and romantic imagination often produced him remarkable adventures, here fell deeply in love. In fact, his head was so stuffed with the machinery and plots of novels and romances, that his heart, as Burns expresses it, "was like a piece of tinder ready to burst forth into a flame, from the first casual spark that might fall upon it." Fortune, however, had as yet guarded it from any such accident, and reserved for winter-quarters and quieter times, the shaft which was to destroy his peace.

He had by dint of application to the principles of the language, and a talent for acquiring it, gained a tolerable knowledge of the Portuguese, and at this time he held a situation which exempted him in a degree from military duty, and left him time to associate with some of the inhabitants who were fond of his conversation, and felt friendly towards him. It was by this means he became acquainted with a female, whose charms had captivated him. She was niece to one of the principal inhabitants, and about fifteen or sixteen years of age. In her he imagined he had found the long-cherished ideal mistress of his soul, on whom he had lavished more accomplishments and perfections than would have made an angel in our degenerate days.

I was, of course, his confidant, and certainly, of all I had ever heard or read of love's extravagance, I witnessed it in him. He could neither eat nor sleep; every spare moment that he had was spent on a small eminence opposite the house where she lived, gazing at the windows, in hopes to catch a glance at her; here he would sit luxuriating in all the wild uncertainty of hope, anticipation, and despair, which lovers commonly indulge in, and although his familiarity with the family might have gained him access to her company any time he pleased, he grew diffident of visiting them, and even shrunk from the idea of speaking to herself on the subject. He poured all his doubts and hopes in my ear, and he could not have found one to whom they were more interesting. Of the same romantic temperament, I shared in all his sensations.

Seeing the state of mind in which he was placed by his violent attachment, I recommended him strongly that he should endeavour to gain an interview, and speak to her on the subject; but he considered this impracticable, as the sight of her never failed to agitate him in such a manner, that it robbed him of all power of utterance. Thus situated, and willing to render my friend a service, through my interest with a family whom she was in the habit of visiting, I brought about an interview between the parties; and here, for the first time, I saw Maria. She was certainly a pretty, good-humoured, lively girl, but in my opinion, very far indeed, from the paragon of perfection which Henry was inclined to think her; but I felt not the magic influence of that power, which, like the philosopher's stone, can transmute the baser metals into gold.

Little satisfaction accrued to Henry from this meeting, but it subsequently led to others in which the parties came to a mutual explanation, and he had reason to hope that he was not regarded by her with indifference. From this time their interviews were more frequent and less guarded; and visiting her aunt frequently, although he could not converse freely with Maria, still their eyes, which "looked unutterable things," were not sufficiently restrained, and the old lady began to suspect the truth; the tattle of the village confirmed her suspicions, and she forbade Henry the house. They had a few stolen meetings at her friend's in the village, but this also was discovered, and Maria was prohibited from leaving the house unattended.

I am almost persuaded that had affairs gone on smoothly, Henry would have come to his senses, and the attachment would have died a natural death. But these obstacles only served to increase his ardour and perseverance; for so well was Maria now guarded, that there was no possibility of seeing her. In this dilemma, he determined on applying to Donna Anna, the girl's aunt; from this application he had but little to hope, yet still he could lose nothing.

Having thus resolved, he went boldly into the house, and without speaking to anyone, lest they might frustrate his purpose, he traversed the passages, until he perceived Donna Anna in one of the apartments alone, employed at her distaff. He entered, his heart fluttering with suspense; and after apologizing for his rudeness in thus intruding upon her, he proceeded to declare his love for Maria, and to beg her acquiescence to their union. The old lady seemed thunderstruck at his presumption, yet still Henry had so qualified his address to her, that she had no good reason to be angry, and after taking a few minutes to recollect herself, she replied, that "Maria was already betrothed to a very deserving young man, a cousin of her own; but independent of this engagement, she could not give her consent. What had Maria to expect if she married a soldier of a foreign regiment? In the midst of war, the soldiers themselves suffered much, but those hardships and sufferings must fall heavier on a delicate female who had never known anything but comfort. No," continued she, "Maria has superior expectations. But supposing I considered you a fit match for her in every other respect, still your religion would be an insurmountable barrier—to enter into the bonds of matrimony with a heretic, she might as well ally herself to the devil! I have no objection to your character, and feel a friendship for you, but I can never encourage you in your present designs, nor give my consent to a marriage, that would be productive of misery to at least one, if not to both parties."

The calm and decided tone in which she spoke, convinced Henry that he had nothing to hope for from her, and his heart grew too big for utterance. He tried to suppress his feelings, but they were too strong for him, and he was only relieved from their suffocating effect by a flood of tears. The Donna's heart softened to see his distress, yet she still remained inflexible to her purpose. Maria, who had seen Henry enter the house, having followed him to the door of her aunt's apartment, had overheard the conversation, and now, seeing her aunt's back turned towards the door, she watched him until he raised his eyes, when giving him a sign which infused new hope into his mind, she retired. Henry now took his leave without enforcing his suit any farther. I had been waiting his return, and when he told me the result of his visit, I encouraged him to hope that all might yet be well.

During the day he received a message by a Portuguese boy, who was servant with one of our officers, informing him that she was so closely watched, that there was no hope of her being able to see him, unless he could manage to get over the garden wall, which was exceedingly high; if so, that she would meet him that night. Having returned an answer that she might expect him, he called upon me; we reconnoitred the garden wall, and having noted where there was a ladder, and procured a rope which was intended for our descent, after waiting anxiously until within half an hour of the appointed time, we proceeded to the place where we intended to effect our escalade.

The inhabitants having retired to rest, and the village silent, we got over without difficulty. We had waited for some time at the head of one of the sidewalks (the place appointed) concealed by the bushes, when we heard the gentle sound of footsteps. We did not move from our hiding-place until the appointed signal was given, when, in an instant, they were in each other's arms.

Where the heart is pure, I am led to believe, that the zest of love is the higher, the lower the station of the lovers. No fictitious refinement interferes to check the cup of joy: so it was in the present instance. Still, however, our situation was perilous, and I urged the necessity of forming some plan to bring about the desired purpose; but their hearts were too much fluttered with joy and hope, uncertainty and fear, to make the necessary arrangements, and they parted hurriedly without doing more than appointing a second meeting.

The appointed time again arrived, and we reached the garden as easily as before, but Maria did not come for nearly an hour after the time agreed on, and we were beginning to think some accident had befallen her, when we heard her steps coming up the walk. She seemed much disturbed; "You would wonder at my delay," said she, "but I am afraid they suspect me. My aunt did not retire to rest at the usual hour, and before she did, she came into my apartment, and held the candle close to my face, but I pretended to sleep soundly; she then retired, and I embraced the opportunity of slipping out—but I cannot stay—she may return to my apartment, and if she does, I am undone."

"But can we come to no conclusion with regard to what should be done?" said I. "You have no reason to hope that your aunt will ever consent to your marriage; therefore your only plan is to escape with Henry, and get married by the chaplain of the division, before your friends can prevent it; then, when they find that no better can be done, there is every reason to believe they will be reconciled to you."

"O it is impossible!" said she; "I know them too well."

"Certainly," said I, "the sacrifice is great, but the alternative is to bid each other *adieu* forever. You must now decide, or we may never have another opportunity."

"I cannot make up my mind tonight," said she; " I will meet

you here tomorrow night at this hour, determined and ready prepared either to remain, or make my escape. Now farewell, for I am afraid that I am discovered."

So saying, she parted hastily from us, and returned into the house, leaving poor Henry in no enviable state; his fate hung upon her decision, she had spoken with uncertainty, and he looked forward to the next meeting as the die that would determine his future happiness or misery.

During the next day, Henry's mind was in such a state of uneasiness and suspense, that I could, with great difficulty, bring him to make the necessary arrangements in the event of her escaping with him. It was necessary that he should apply to his commanding officer for permission to marry; and I advised him to disclose the whole matter to him, well knowing that such a character as he was would take an interest in his fate.

Henry took my advice, and having called on Colonel L—— disclosed every circumstance connected with the affair. Colonel L—— listened with attention, and seemed much interested. The story in part was not new to him; he had heard it from some of the principal inhabitants. He reasoned the matter with Henry like a father; represented the difficulty which would lie in his path—marrying a foreigner of a different religion—the hardships she would have to endure—and the many difficulties which two people, marrying so young, would have to encounter. "But," said he, " I suppose all those things appear as trifles to you at present."

Henry owned that his affection was too deeply rooted to be moved by these considerations.

"Well," said Colonel L——, "if you are determined on trying the experiment, and that she is agreeable, I have no objection to giving you permission to marry, but I cannot say you have my approbation."

Henry, however, it may be easily imagined, was not to be moved by sober reasoning. The time of meeting arrived, and Henry, trembling with suspense and apprehension, accompanied me to the garden. We were not long there, when Maria arrived with a few articles of wearing apparel, which she had hurriedly collected.

"Well, Maria," said I, "have you decided—are you ready to accompany us?"

"I don't know," said she, "I am so filled with apprehension, that I cannot think or speak."

"Say the word," said I, "all is ready."

"Oh, I don't know," said she. "Either let me return into the house, or let us leave this, or I shall die with fear: I am sure I have been observed. O Jesu, Maria! there they come—I am lost."

So saying, she fled down the opposite path, where she was immediately seized by some of the domestics, who had been mustered for the purpose of surprising us. There was no time to lose, for resistance would have been useless; and we too well knew the nature of the Portuguese, to depend much on their mercy. Hurrying, therefore, towards the wall, and having assisted Henry, who was rendered nearly powerless by the effect of his feelings, I made a spring and seized the top of the wall; Henry was ready to lend me assistance, but before I could get myself raised to the summit, a sword aimed for my body, struck the wall so close to my side, that it cut out a piece of my jacket and shirt. Ere the blow could be repeated, I had fallen over on the opposite side, carrying Henry with me in my fall. I was severely hurt—but there was no time to lose, and we knew the alarm would soon be raised; therefore, having conveyed the ladder to where we had found it, we hurried to our quarters.

Next day the Portuguese boy brought information to Henry that early that morning two mules had been brought into the courtyard; that Maria was brought out weeping, and mounted on one, her aunt on the other, and that two servants, armed, had accompanied them; he was not allowed to follow them, and therefore could not tell what direction they had taken, but Maria had whispered to him, to give Henry her last farewell, for she never expected to see him again, as she was ignorant of where they were taking her.

When Henry received this information, distracted with a

thousand contending emotions, among which despair was predominant, he seized a bayonet, and rushed bare-headed from his quarters, traversed one road after another in search of her, making inquiry of every person whom he met, if they had seen her—but she had been some hours gone. After travelling about from one place to another in this distracted state, and being taken for a madman by all who met him, worn out by the violence of his feelings, he became calm, and returned home in the dusk of the evening; but it was a calm produced by one master feeling having swallowed up the rest; despair had now taken possession of his mind, "The stricken bosom that can sigh, no mortal arrow bears."

He walked into his apartment, and having taken up a musket, and loaded it, he placed the muzzle against his head, and was in the act of putting his foot on the trigger, when a soldier happened to enter, and seizing him, arrested the rash deed.

I had been placed on guard that morning, nor did I know anything of what had occurred until Henry was brought to the guard-house, where he was ordered to be particularly watched. I went over to speak to him, but he looked at me with a vacant stare, nor did he seem conscious of what I said. Sitting down in a corner, he remained with his eyes fixed on the floor for some time, then rising, he walked about with a hurried pace, while his countenance showed the burning fever of his mind; a fit of tenderness succeeded, and he raved of all that had happened, which I only could understand.

To me it was a most affecting scene, for I had no hope that his reason would return, and I contemplated the wreck of his mind, as one would do the destruction of all that was dear to him. I watched him attentively during the night, and towards morning nature became so far exhausted, that he fell into a confused slumber. When he awoke, the naked reality of his situation struck him intensely. He perceived me, and stretching out his hand, he burst into tears. In broken accents he informed me of the death of all his hopes; but his mind was unstrung—he could not think connectedly.

At this time he was sent for to attend at the colonel's lodgings. The noble character of our commanding officer was particularly shown in the sympathy and concern which he evinced for the unfortunate Henry: he entered into all his feelings, and alternately soothed and reasoned with him, until he had brought him to a calmer state of mind; then, after expressing the kindest solicitude for his welfare, he dismissed him to his quarters, telling him at the same time, that he would use his interest to gain the consent of her relations to the match, and that nothing should be wanting on his part to bring the affair to a happy conclusion.

This, in some measure, restored the balm of hope to Henry's mind; but, alas! it was only a temporary relief, for although Colonel L———. faithfully kept his promise, and several of the officers who were on good terms with the family used their utmost endeavours in his behalf, it was all to no purpose—the more they pressed, the more obstinate they became.

Things were in this state, when he unexpectedly received a message from Maria, informing him that she was closely confined in the house of a gentleman, (who was a relative of her aunt,) about nine miles from the town; from the manner in which she was guarded, she had no hope of being able to make her escape, for there were people employed to watch the avenues to the house, with orders if he approached it to show him no mercy; that she saw little use in giving him this information, but she could not resist the opportunity which had presented itself, of letting him know where she was. Henry gave way to the most entrancing anticipations on receiving this information; but when he communicated it to me, I considered the subject in a different light. I saw that it was more likely to keep alive the commotion of a passion which there was little hope of ever arriving at its object; I knew the attempt to go to the house would be pregnant with danger, still I felt inclined to assist him in another determinate effort to carry off the prize.

Henry called on Colonel L——— for the purpose of procuring a pass. When he communicated his intention, he not only gave him the pass, but also a letter to the gentleman of the house where Maria was, (with whom he was well acquainted,) to serve as an introduction. Thus prepared, Henry and I, in company with the boy already mentioned, set forward after it was dark towards the place, taking a by-road.

When we reached the house, we left the boy outside, as he was known to the family, and entering, presented the letter from Colonel L———. We were kindly received; and as it was late, the gentleman insisted on us stopping all night—so far all was well. We had been about an hour in the house when Maria happened to come downstairs: she knew us immediately, but concealed her emotion, and coming near the fire, she watched for an opportunity when the servants were engaged about the house, and then whispering to us, asked our motive in coming there. "If they know you," said she, "your lives are not safe."

I told her that our motive was by some means to endeavour to effect her escape; she replied, it was utterly impossible, she was too well guarded. "Farewell, Henry," said she, "farewell forever, for I believe I will never see you again; it would have been happy for us both if we had never seen each other."

At this moment a female servant of Donna Anna's, who had accompanied Maria, came to speak to her, and recognising Henry, she flew upstairs. Maria saw that we were discovered, and she cried to us, "Fly for your lives!"

The whole family collected, were now descending the stairs, and Maria was hurried up to her room. The old lady of the house assailed us with the most abusive epithets, the men-servants gathered in, and everything wore a hostile appearance. The gentleman, however, to whom the letter was directed, commanded silence, and addressing us, "I do not presume to say what your intentions may be towards my ward, but being convinced of the identity of the individual who has already caused us so much trouble, I am forced, even against the laws of hospitality, to retract my request of you to remain here tonight, and for the safety of those committed to my charge, I must insist on you returning immediately to your quarters. If you have come here for the purpose of decoying Maria from this house, I can tell you that whatever inclination she once might have felt for this foolish young man, she is now better advised, and does not wish to be troubled with him any more."

"Let me hear that from her own lips," cried Henry in a frenziedly tone, "and I will give my word that I shall never trouble her again."

A short consultation was held by the family, and after some minutes delay, Maria was brought downstairs, trembling and weeping. But all their endeavours could not force her to repeat the words which they wished her to say. At length, Henry, as if inspired with more than his natural energy, exclaimed, "I find that every fresh effort of mine only causes you additional restraint and mortification. I must now cease to hope—they have cruelly parted us in this world, Maria, but we may yet meet. Suffer me," said he, "to take a last farewell, and I will trouble you no more."

This was spoken with such an impassioned voice and gesture, that it had a visible effect on those around. Maria, who had been restrained by the lady of the house, now broke from her, and fell into Henry's arms. While he pressed her to his bosom, a new spirit seemed to animate him—his eyes brightened—and putting his hand into his breast, where he had a pistol concealed, "Let us carry her off, Joseph," said he to me in English, "or die in the attempt."

"Then you will die before you reach the door," said I; for the house was now filled with retainers of the family; and as if they suspected his purpose, Maria was torn shrieking from his arms.

Afraid that he might be induced to commit some rash act, I hurried him out of the house, and we returned home. I endeavoured to lead him into conversation, but he appeared not to hear me, nor did he speak a word during the journey; he evinced no feeling of any kind—his mind seemed to be in a state of the utmost confusion.

Next morning the Portuguese boy brought him intelligence that Maria had passed through the village very early, escorted by her relations, on her way to a nunnery, about three leagues distant, where she was destined to remain until our army advanced.

This took place in a few days after, and they never met again. Henry's mind had been strained far beyond its pitch—it was now unnerved—and he fell into a state of listless melancholy from which he did not recover for many months.

CHAPTER 19

Vittoria

During the time the army were in winter quarters, great preparations were made for the campaign which was about to open, and we could now muster an army of about one hundred and thirty thousand men, namely, forty thousand British, twenty thousand Portuguese, and seventy thousand Spaniards—the two former in the highest state of discipline, well clothed, and provided with stores of every description. The old camp-kettles, that were formerly carried on mules, were exchanged for lighter ones, which the men could carry on the top of their knapsacks; and the mules now carried tents, which we had not been provided with prior to this period. In fact, the whole arrangements made reflected the highest honour on Lord Wellington.

The army commenced its advance on the 13th May, 1813, in three columns. The second division commanded by General Hill, formed the right, which was destined to advance along the line of the Tagus. The centre column, consisting of the fourth, sixth, seventh, and light divisions, under the immediate command of Lord Wellington, to advance by Salamanca. The left, consisting of the first, third, and fifth divisions, under the command of General Graham, to advance direct through Portugal, taking the line of the Benevente for Burgos, and to be supported on the left by the Gallician army. The centre column came up with the French on the 26th May, and in a skirmish with their rear-guard, took two hundred prisoners.

A junction was here formed with General Hill, extending

the line from the Tormes to the Douro. The left, to which our division belonged, passed the Elsa at Miranda de Douro on the 31st May, Lord Wellington being present, and advanced upon Zamora, when the French fell back upon Toro. Passing Valladolid, we continued our march upon Burgos, which the enemy evacuated on the 13th of June, having first blown up the works; thirty of the garrison perished by the explosion.

The retreat of the French had been so rapid during this time, that our marches were often very severe, which, together with the heat of the weather, and occasional scarcity of water, caused many to get fatigued, and unable to keep up with their regiment. Here again the conduct of Colonel Lloyd was remarkable. By every means in his power he encouraged and assisted those who were weakly, taking their knapsacks from them, and carrying them on his own horse; sometimes having half a dozen on it, and a man sitting above all, while he walked on foot at the head of his regiment, in the most difficult parts of the road—at the same time, inducing the other officers to follow his example. Often when he saw an individual failing, through want of strength, he has taken off his liquor-flask and given it to the poor fellow to drink, saying, "Don't let your spirits down, my man; you will soon get strength, and be able to keep up with the best of them; none of them shall have to say that you fell to the rear."

He had a most extensive and thorough knowledge of his profession, added to an acquaintance with most of the European languages. When he came into camp he was never a moment idle, either reconnoitring the enemy's position, or drawing charts of the roads, &c. He scarcely allowed himself to rest, and was always up an hour or two before the bugle sounded; but he would never allow the men to be disturbed before the proper time. "No," said he, "let the poor fellows get all the rest they can." But then he expected them to be alert; officers and men, without distinction, were obliged to be in their respective places at once without delay—all his motions were double-quick—and he detested nothing so much as laziness.

General Picton, who had joined from England a considerable time before, again commanded the division. To judge from appearance, no one would have suspected him of humour; yet he often indulged in it: his wit was generally, however, of the satirical kind. On this advance, a man belonging to one of the regiments of the brigade, who was remarkable for his mean pilfering disposition, had on some pretence lingered behind his regiment when they marched out to the assembling ground, and was prowling about from one house to another in search of plunder. General Picton, who was passing through, happened to cast his eye upon him, and called out, "What are you doing there, sir? Why are you behind your regiment?"

The man, who did not expect to see the general in the village, had not an answer very ready; but he stammered out an excuse, saying, "I came back to the house where I was quartered to look for my gallowses," (braces).

"I see how it is," replied the general; "get along, sir, to your division, and take my advice—always keep the word *gallows* in your mind."

Having crossed the Ebro on the 16th, Lord Wellington took up his quarters a few leagues from Vittoria; and on the 19th we came up with the French, who had taken a position in front of that town, their left posted on a range of heights. Our army having closed up on the 20th, on the morning of the 21st, General Hill's division commenced the battle, by attacking their left on the heights of Puebla, and succeeded, after a most desperate and sanguinary contest, in gaining possession of them. When we descended the hill towards the river, the second division was warmly engaged, and the French commenced cannonading us from a small white village in front of Vittoria, where they had part of their army stationed.

There was a brigade of our guns directing their fire towards this place when we were crossing the river along with the seventh division. Our attention was drawn to a young artillery officer who was with them, and who seemed to be very much frightened; for every time that either our own or the French guns fired, he ducked to the ground. Some of the men felt inclined to make game of him; but it only showed that fighting needs practice before people can take things easy. It is likely that it was the first time he had been engaged, and I have no doubt but he would eventually get the better of that custom.

Those who have not known it by experience, can form no idea of the indifference with which our soldiers entered a battle after being some time in the Peninsula. As an instance of this, we were at one time lying opposite to the enemy, in daily expectation of being engaged. One of our men, (a Highlandman,) having lost the small piece of ornamented leather which is worn in front of the uniform cap, on taking off his hat for some purpose, the deficiency caught his eye, and, looking at it for a few moments, he said, very seriously, "I wish to God there may be an engagement today, till I get a rosette for my cap."

After crossing the river, our division advanced in two lines upon the village where their artillery were posted under a tremendous fire, and succeeded, after an obstinate resistance, in dislodging them. The fourth and light divisions having also crossed the river, advanced upon the enemy's centre. The French had made sure of defeating us at this point; and it was said that Joseph Bonaparte had erected a buttress on one of the spires, for the purpose of seeing them drive us back. But he was doomed to a severe disappointment; for the second division having succeeded in driving the French off the heights, they commenced their retreat on the Burgos road, but were intercepted by General Graham, with the left of our army; and after losing several villages in succession, which they warmly contested, they were at length compelled to abandon the main road to France, (Joseph himself narrowly escaping,) and take the road to Pampeluna, followed in pursuit by the whole army; and such was their haste, that they were obliged to abandon all their baggage and guns, with the exception of one gun and one howitzer.

One hundred and fifty-one cannon, four hundred and fifteen ammunition wagons, one hundred other wagons, fourteen thousand rounds of ammunition, two million ball cartridges, and forty thousand pounds of powder, with the baggage and treasury wagons, said to be worth 630,000*l.*, fell into our hands.

The enemy lost ten thousand killed and wounded, and one thousand nine hundred prisoners. The loss on our side amounted to about three thousand killed and wounded.

When we reached the town, passing to the left of it, we found their baggage to the right of the road, lying in the greatest confusion. The columns passed on, but some of the stragglers who fell out got immense sums of money out of the treasury wagons. Few of them were much the better of it, however. I knew one man who got to the amount of £2000 here, who was going without shoes before we left the country. We passed on some distance beyond Vittoria, and encamped; but many of the men returned that night to the baggage, and got money and valuables of every description. The camp that night and next day was like a fair; and the dollars and doubloons were flying about in every direction.

The wounded were left in Vittoria, among whom was a Captain G—— of ours, who subsequently lost his life in a melancholy manner. During his stay in Vittoria, while recovering from his wounds, he had become acquainted with a young lady, and, it was said, had seduced her. Her brother, who was an officer in the Spanish army, having learned the circumstance, vowed revenge; and one night, when on guard, he took some of his men with him armed, and forced his way into Captain G——'s quarters, who was undressing himself to go to bed. Hearing a noise, he seized his sword, and coming out into the passage, he was attacked by the Spaniards; but so well did he defend himself, that they were fairly beaten out of the house, and the door shut upon them. They had not been long gone, however, when they returned, and endeavoured to gain entrance.

Captain G—— had again left his apartment to see what was the matter, and was standing in the passage with his sword in his hand, when they burst open the door, fired a volley at him, and made their escape. One of the shots took effect, and he fell mortally wounded. We were very sorry for him, for he was an excellent officer; and however he might have been to blame otherwise, the base manner in which he was assassinated excited the indignation of the whole army. I never learned whether any investigation took place, or any justice was rendered by the Spanish government.

The rear of the French army entered Pampeluna on the 24th, having previously lost their gun; and out of their whole artillery, they had now only left one solitary howitzer. Never was an army so discomfited. They were so confident of success, that they had made no provision for a retreat.

Having left a garrison in Pampeluna, they proceeded to retreat by the road of Roncesvalles, and we invested Pampeluna on the 26th. We were in camp for a day or two here; and during that time, a party of our regiment relieved a Spanish picket on a hill above our encampment. It had rained during the night, and the picket's arms, which were piled in front of the tent, had got a little rusty. Being fatigued, they had neglected to clean them. Colonel Lloyd, who was ever on the alert, particularly when near the enemy, having paid them a visit very early in the morning, took notice of their arms; but, without passing any remark, he called the sergeant, who, thinking that he wished to inspect the picket, ordered them to turn out.

"Never mind falling in," said the colonel; "I only called to ask why you did not make those Spaniards whom you relieved last night take their arms with them."

The sergeant, who did not see through the sarcasm, replied, that the Spaniards did take their arms with them.

"And pray, whose arms are these?"

"The picket's arms," replied the sergeant.

"Poh! nonsense! you don't intend to make me believe these arms belong to British soldiers? Send for the Spaniards, and make them take away their arms." So saying, he walked down the hill.

Each man felt his honour implicated, and the colonel had not gone many paces when they were all busy cleansing their muskets. It was in this manner that he could convey severe reproof, and endear himself to his men at the same time.

From this place we marched across the country to Sanguessa, and on the march I was left on duty, which detained me behind the regiment. In my route to join them, I had halted for the day with my party at a house a short distance off the road. There was a wood to the rear of the house, and we had not long taken up our quarters, when I perceived a lady galloping from it with great speed down a by-path towards us. As she approached, I observed that her dress was in great disorder, her face stained with blood, and she held a pistol in her hand, with which she urged on her horse.

I was struck with surprise on seeing a lady in such trim, and did not know well what to think of her, when she reined up her horse at the door, and before I had time to assist her, sprung to the ground, and replacing the pistol in the holster, removed the saddle from her horse, and turned him loose to graze; then sitting down, she drew forth a small pocket mirror, and began to arrange her dishevelled tresses. As a favour she asked me to procure her a little water, and when I had brought it—"Thank you," said she, "I believe I stand in need of this, for I have had a severe scuffle and a brisk gallop. I am on my way to join the Spanish army, and although eager to get forward, I could not persuade my lazy servants to dispense with their usual siesta, and when the fellows went to sleep I left them and pushed forward myself; but I had not travelled far when I was stopped by three brigands, who, seizing my horse's bridle, demanded my money. Powder and shot are more plentiful with me than money in these times, and I drew out a pistol and sent a ball through the fellow's head who asked it—he fell, and I urged forward my horse; but one of the villains still held by the bridle, and I was near unhorsed. Having another pistol left, I lost no time in making him relax his hold. My horse was now free, and sprung forward with me; but a bullet from the surviving robber nearly stopped my flight, for it grazed my cheek here," said she, pointing to a slight wound which she was bathing with the cold water: "it was a narrow escape, certainly."

I was not a little surprised at the *sang froid* with which she described the imminent danger she had been in, and could not sufficiently admire her courage and presence of mind; but I ceased to wonder, when her servants coming up a short time after, told me that I had been conversing with the heroine of Saragossa.

In half an hour after they arrived, she again set forward. I had seen her before at Cadiz; but I did not recollect her features. Everyone has read or heard of her conduct at Saragossa; it will, therefore, be needless for me to recapitulate it here.

Having remained in camp at Sanguesa a few days, we returned, and were quartered in a small village, called Olaz, about three miles from Pampeluna, sending out working parties to the batteries which were forming against the town.

General Graham having pushed on by the sea-side as far as Passages, and General Hill having dislodged the enemy on the right—the whole had now retired into France.

We remained in this place until the 20th of August, when Soult having hastily collected an army of forty thousand men, made a furious attack on the fourth division. Our division advanced to their support, but not being able to keep our ground against such a force as they had brought up, the whole were obliged to retreat precipitately that night upon Huarte, where a position was taken up by the army.

On the 27th they made a desperate attack on the left of our line, where we had possession of a hill, which they made repeated attempts to gain possession of, but without success—for whenever they drove in our skirmishers, so as to reach the top, the regiments stationed to defend it came forward, and having poured a volley into them, charged them down the hill with dreadful slaughter.

On the 28th they again attempted it, but with like success. A desperate attack was then made on the fourth division, but they charged with the bayonet, and repulsed the enemy with immense loss. On the 29th Soult manoeuvred to turn our left; but on the 30th, our army in turn attacked—the seventh division their right, our division their left, and the other divisions their centre—when they were defeated and fled in all directions, losing in their retreat many prisoners, among whom were a number of raw conscripts, who had not been four months enlisted.

During the time we lay in position, the French occupied a hill on one side, while our division were posted on a rise opposite, a small valley being between; in this valley there was a sort of entrenchment formed, where our pickets lay. It could be of little use to either side, as it was exposed to the fire of both armies; but the French, out of bravado, determined on taking it, and selected a party for that purpose. A brave fellow of an officer headed them, and came cheering down the hill; our men did not incommode themselves in the least, until they were so near that they could take a sure aim, when those in the rear of the entrenchment starting up, saluted them with a volley of musketry that brought down an immense number, among others the officer, who was some way in front; when they saw him fall, they turned to the right-about, and ascended the hill, leaving him on the ground. We felt sorry for the fate of the brave fellow who had led them, and reprehended the cowardly scoundrels who had left him.

It is a peculiar feature of the British soldier, that his bravery does not depend on that of his officers, although, no doubt, it may be stimulated by the presence and example of a good one—I never knew it to fail through their bad conduct.

From this we followed the French by the road of Roncesvalles, and took up our encampment on one of the Pyrenees, above that village so much renowned in Spanish poetry. In our ascent we found a number of half-burnt bodies lying on the mountainside, being those of the enemy who had been killed in the preceding engagement, and whom they thus disposed of. When we reached the top of the hill, we found ourselves enveloped in mist; and during the few days we remained on it, it was so thick that we durst not move from the camp for water, without forming a chain of men to guide us back. From this place we removed, and were posted on the heights above the village of Maya, occupying the ground from which part of our advanced posts were driven back on the 25th; the scene of action being marked out by the dead bodies lying about, and the ground strewed with the fragments of clothing, particularly the tartan-dress of one of our Highland regiments.

Being relieved by other troops, we descended the mountain, and we were encamped near the village of Ariscune. While here, one of the 83rd regiment was shot for desertion; he had deserted when we formed the advance at the Maya Pass, and having come out with some of the French generals to reconnoitre our position, they were attacked by a picket of our cavalry, when the French officers decamped, leaving the deserter behind. He was then taken, and being subsequently tried by a general court-martial, was sentenced to be shot. He blamed the tyrannical conduct of the officer commanding his company, and the pay-sergeant, for being the cause of his desertion—that they had taken ill-will at him on some account, and rendered his life so miserable, that he was driven to the desperate step which ended in his death. Whether his statement was true, I cannot say, but his comrades were inclined to think it was.

During this time General Graham besieged and took St. Sebastian.

While we were here, I was sent on command with a letter to General Hill, whose division now occupied the heights above Roncesvalles. In going from the one place to the other, I had to travel about six miles through a by-path, on the ridge of one of the Pyrenees, and my imagination was struck in a peculiar manner by the awful grandeur of the scenery; yet I could not help feeling horror at the deathlike stillness that reigned around me. I felt myself as it were lifted out of the world—I saw nor heard not any living thing but a huge vulture, who stood upright on a rock by the roadside, looking at me as I passed, without seeming the least disturbed at my presence—he rather seemed to eye me as an invader of his solitary domain. I tried to startle him by making a noise, but he disdained to move; at length, when it suited his own pleasure, he slowly expanded his broad wings, and rising a few yards from the ground, hovered for some time immediately above my head, and then soared out of sight.

Having ascended the mountain, I found the second division encamped on nearly the same ground that we had formerly occupied, and enveloped in mist as we had been. The place where General Hill and his staff were encamped was surrounded by a small entrenchment, inside of which the tents were pitched, and a kind of log-house built in the centre, to serve as a mess-room.

Judging from the proud and haughty bearing of some of our ensigns, in coming into the presence of the general second in command of the British army, I expected to be annihilated by his look, and I was ushered into the mess-room to deliver my message with a palpitating heart; but I no sooner saw the humane and benevolent-looking countenance of the general, than my apprehensions vanished. Having read the letter, he questioned me concerning the health of the commanding officer, and asked me questions concerning our regiment, (of which he was colonel,) in the kindliest and most unaffected manner; then calling one of his servants, he ordered him to provide me liberally in meat and drink. Some time after, seeing me standing outside the tent, he called me, and asked whether the servants had paid attention to me.

Next morning, on giving me a letter for my commanding officer, "I did not intend," said he, "that you should have returned so soon, but we are going to remove down to the valley, and as it would be only taking you out of your road, it will be as well for you to proceed; but there is no necessity that you should go farther than the small village two leagues from this I will give directions to my orderly dragoon to procure you a billet there, and tomorrow you can join your regiment." He then ordered his servant to fill my haversack with provision; and when I was going away, he said, "Remember now what I have told you—don't go farther than the village; and here is something for you to get yourself a refreshment when you arrive there."

These circumstances have no particular interest in themselves, to render them worth reciting, only that they serve to show the amiable disposition of a general, whose character for bravery and skill is too well known to the public to need any eulogium of mine It was this feeling and humane disposition, and attention to their interests, that caused him to be so much beloved by the troops under his command, and gained for him the appellation of father—"Daddy Hill" being the name he was called by in his division.

CHAPTER 20

Crossing the Bidasoa

From Ariscune we again moved, and occupied the heights above Maya, from whence we advanced in the beginning of October, and drove the French outposts back into the valley, at the same time burning their huts. While engaged at this business, there fell a tremendous shower of hailstones, some of them measuring five inches in circumference. The regiment got partially under cover in a small chapel, but those with the baggage were exposed, and many were hurt severely. On this day the left of our army succeeded in crossing the Bidasoa.

On returning from this affair, we ascended the heights above the village of Zaggaramurdi, where we encamped. From this part of the Pyrenees we had a view of France, and the position of the French army, which occupied a line, their right resting on the seaport of St. Jean de Luz, and the left on St. Jean Pied de Port: here they had formed an entrenched camp, and had redoubts on each hill along the whole line.

We remained on this ground until the 10th of November, during which time the weather was severe—the wind often blowing with such violence that the tents could not be kept pitched.

From a precipice above our encampment, we could view the sea, and the towns along the coast. It was now three years since we beheld it, during which time our hopes and wishes had often fondly turned to our native homes; each fresh campaign and each battle was reckoned the precursor of our return, but "by expectation every day beguiled," we had almost begun to despair of ever beholding it again, when our recent successes, and the sight of the ocean which encircled the land of our birth, produced the most lively hopes and pleasing anticipations. A more than common friendly feeling was displayed amongst us; each saw in his comrade's face the reflection of the joy that animated his own heart. The mountain air braced our nerves, and gave us a bounding elasticity of spirit, which rose superior to everything.

A few of us who were drawn together by congeniality of sentiment and disposition, used to assemble and wander up among the giant cliffs with which we were surrounded, and perching ourselves in a cranny, would sit gazing on the ocean and ships passing, with emotions which I have felt, but cannot describe. Its expansive bosom seemed a magic mirror, wherein we could read our future fortune—a happy return from all our dangers; smiling friends, with all the early loved associations of childhood and youth, swam before our hope-dazzled imaginations, and we sat and sung the songs of Scotland while the tears trickled down our cheeks. He who has never heard the melodies of his native land sung in a foreign country, is ignorant of a pleasure that nothing can surpass. But we were not all doomed to realize those pleasing anticipations: many found their graves in the valley which we then overlooked.

Lord Wellington having prepared everything for an attack on the French position in the valley, on the 10th of November, about two o'clock in the morning, we assembled, and having marched down to the foot of the hill, on a signal given by a gun firing, the attack commenced; that on the enemy's kit was made under the direction of General Hill, by the second and sixth divisions, supported by a division of Portuguese and Spaniards. Marshal Beresford commanded the centre, consisting of our division, the fourth and seventh, supported by a division of Spaniards.

The enemy having been driven from the redoubts in front of Sarre, we advanced upon the village. Our regiment being selected to charge a strong column that protected the bridge,

Colonel Lloyd filed us off from the division, and led us on to the attack in the most heroic manner. Having succeeded in carrying it with considerable loss on our part, we returned and took up our place in the column. In a short time after, having passed through the village, the whole army cooperating, we advanced to the attack of the enemy's main position on the heights behind it, on which a line of strong redoubts were formed, with abattis in front, formed by trees cut down and placed with their branches towards us, serving as a cover for their infantry.

Having extended our line at the foot of the hill, our division proceeded to the attack: Colonel Lloyd having pushed his horse forward before the regiment, advanced cheering on his men with the most undaunted bravery—but before he reached its summit, he received a mortal wound in the breast, and was only saved from falling off his horse by some of the men springing forward to his assistance. When this was perceived by the regiment, a pause of a moment was made in the midst of their career, and the tear started into each eye as they saw him borne down the hill; but the next was devoted to revenge, and regardless of everything, they broke through all obstacles, and driving the enemy from their position, they charged them through their burning huts without mercy. The troops to our right and left having carried the other redoubts, the enemy were obliged to surrender the strong position which they had taken; and in the principal redoubt on the right, they left the first battalion of their 88th regiment, which surrendered.

The troops under General Hill having succeeded in forcing them from their positions on the right of our army, our division and the seventh moved by the left of the Nivelle, on St. Pe, covered by the second and sixth divisions. A part of the enemy's troops had crossed, and advancing, gained possession of the height above it. Our centre and right columns were now established behind the enemy's right; but night came on, and we were obliged to cease firing.

Having encamped, intelligence was brought up of the death of Colonel Lloyd: he had been carried to a house at the foot of the hill, where he expired in a few minutes. Thus fell the brave and noble Lloyd, in the vigour of manhood and the height of his fame, for his worth and services were well known, and duly appreciated by Lord Wellington. Though young, his extraordinary abilities had caused him to rise rapidly in the service, and had attracted the admiration of the army in which he served; while his humanity and wise system of discipline endeared him to those he commanded. Humble though thy grave be, gallant Lloyd, and though no sculptured marble rises o'er thy tomb, thine is a nobler meed: thy virtues are engraven on many a heart, which nothing but the rude hand of death can e'er efface; and though no pageantry followed thy remains to the grave, honest heartfelt tears were shed upon it.

I never witnessed sorrow so general as that produced by the intelligence of his death; our hearts were full—we felt as if we had lost a father—all his good qualities were recapitulated, and tears were shed in abundance during the recital.

Had any of those overbearing officers who carry all with a high hand and by dint of severity, witnessed the feelings displayed that night among the men of our regiment, they would have forsworn tyranny forever. One individual only exulted in his death, and that was the captain of yellow and black badge celebrity, whom I have already had occasion to mention; he considered that Colonel Lloyd's promotion into our regiment had hindered his own, and as the goodness which some men cannot imitate causes their hate, so it was with him. When he received intelligence of Colonel Lloyd's death, snapping his fingers in a manner peculiar to himself, he exclaimed, "They have been licking the butter off my bread for some time, but I think I have them now."

This unfeeling expression becoming known in the regiment, caused him more detestation even than his former cruelty.

The enemy retired from the position on their right that night, and quitting also their position and works in front of St. Jean de Luz, retired upon Bidart, destroying the bridges on the lower Nivelle. In the course of the preceding day we had taken fifty-one pieces of cannon, six ammunition tumbrels, and one thousand four hundred prisoners.

In consequence of the rapid movements of the division, the baggage had not come up, and as it rained heavily, we were rather uncomfortably situated. Next day we moved forward a short distance, through dreadfully dirty roads, but the enemy having retired into an entrenched camp before Bayonne, we halted and again encamped, when the baggage joined us. Some of them had been nearly taken by the French during the preceding night; our division being farther advanced than the enemy's right, they were uncertain where to direct their march.

The corporal of our band, a Glasgow lad, coming up that evening with the baggage, observed a poor woman of the 88th regiment endeavouring to raise the ass that carried her necessaries, out of a hole it had fallen into. As it was getting dark, and the baggage had all passed, the poor woman was in a miserable plight, and begged of him to assist her. She could not have applied to one more willing to succour a person in distress, and setting to work, after a good deal of trouble, he got the *borico* on its feet, but so much time had elapsed that the baggage was now out of hearing, and they were uncertain which way to proceed. After travelling some distance, they heard bugles sounding to their left, and they kept on in that direction, until they found themselves in the midst of some regiments of Spaniards, but who could give them no information respecting the position of our division. Pointing, however, to where they suspected them to be, our travellers continued their route in that direction; but the poor ass was so fatigued that it lay down every now and then under its burden. Assisting it on in the best way they could, the road they had taken brought them between two hills, on which they perceived the fires of different encampments. When they arrived opposite them, they suspected from their relative position, that one must be the enemy, but which of them they knew not; they were now in a dilemma, and to add to it, the poor ass tumbled headlong into a stream that ran through the valley, and their united efforts could not raise it.

P——'s spirit of knight-errantry was now fast evaporating, and he was almost tempted to swear that he would never again be caught succouring distressed damsels, when the woman, whose invention was sharpened by the exigency of her situation, proposed that she would creep softly up the hill, until she came within hearing of the soldiers in the camp, and from their language she would be able to learn whether they were our troops or the enemy. She then ascended the hill that she considered the most likely to be the encampment of our troops, leaving poor P—— sitting beside the half-drowned animal, to whose name he was inclined to think the transactions of that night gave him some claim.

After waiting a considerable time in anxious suspense, he was beginning to forget his selfish considerations, in concern for the safety of the poor woman who had thus ventured on a forlorn hope, when his attention was attracted by someone descending the hill waving a light backwards and forwards, and shouting at the same time; having answered the signal, the woman soon made her appearance, with a Portuguese soldier, whose division was encamped on the hill which she ascended, and they now learned that those on the opposite hill were the French.

Having succeeded in raising the half-perished *buro*, the Portuguese lifted the baggage on his back, and the others half dragging, half carrying the animal, they reached the top of the hill, but still no information could be got of the division. Considering it of no use to proceed farther, they seated themselves by a fire, but they had scarcely done so, when it came on a heavy shower of rain which drenched them to the skin—there was no remedy, however, but patience. Next morning at daylight they again took the road, but they were now more fortunate, for falling in with some of the baggage they had parted with the preceding night, they reached the division by the time we had encamped.

During our campaigns in the Peninsula, it is almost incredible what the poor women who followed us had to endure, marching often in a state of pregnancy, and frequently bearing their children in the open air, in some instances, on the line of march, by the roadside; suffering, at the same time, all the privation to which the army was liable. In quarters, on the other hand, they were assailed by every temptation which could be thrown in their way and every scheme laid by those who had rank and money, to rob them of that virtue which was all they had left to congratulate themselves upon.

Was it to be wondered at, then, if many of them were led astray, particularly when it is considered that their starving condition was often taken advantage of by those who had it in their power to supply them, but who were villains enough to make their chastity the price?

From this encampment we advanced to Ustaritz, where we remained until the 9th of December, when we crossed the Nive. At the point we passed, we met with little or no opposition, but some of the army were warmly engaged. We then took up our quarters in Hasparin. The day that we entered this village, one of our men cut off his right hand, under circumstances that may be worth relating.

For some time previous to this he had been low in spirits, troubled with what some people call religious melancholy, but which, at that time, was no very prevalent disease in the army. He scarcely ever spoke to anyone, and was in the habit of wandering out from the encampment, with his Bible in his pocket, and, seating himself in some place where he was not likely to be disturbed, he would sit for hours poring over it. While in Ustaritz, he conceived some ill will against the landlord of the house where he was quartered, and very unceremoniously knocked him down. Being confined for this offence, he remained a prisoner when we entered Hasparin.

On the guard being placed in a house, he sat down, and having taken out his Bible, he commenced reading it. But suddenly rising, he laid down the book, and going over to a man who was breaking wood with a hatchet, he asked the loan of it for a few minutes. When the man gave it to him, he walked very deliberately into an inner apartment, and placing his right hand on the sill of the window, he severed it at the wrist. The first two strokes that he made did not finish the business, and he had nerve enough not only to repeat it a third time, but afterwards to wrench the lacerated integuments asunder, and throw the hand into the court below. He had been observed by some of the men in a window opposite, but too late to prevent the deed.

I assisted in leading him to the assistant-surgeon's quarters, where the stump was dressed in a manner which I shall describe, and leave to the profession either to praise or censure, as they may feel inclined. The bone had been rather splintered than cut, and its sharp points protruded about two inches beyond the mangled integuments. Having prepared his apparatus, he placed the patient on a seat, and after half an hour's poking with a *tenaculum*, he succeeded in taking up and tying the two principal arteries. He then nipped off the rough angles at the point of the bone, and forcing down the retracted integuments by straps of adhesive plaster, under which he had introduced some dry lint, he rolled the whole up with a bandage, and left him, congratulating himself, no doubt, on his dexterity.

The man, on being questioned as to his motive in thus mutilating himself, replied, "that he had only done what the Lord commanded, in a passage he had been reading— *'If thy right hand offend thee, cut it off, and cast it from thee,'* &c., which injunction he had literally fulfilled, as his right hand offended him by knocking down his landlord. This was the only reason ever assigned. As he went to the rear some time after, and did not join the regiment again, I had never an opportunity of learning whether the operation proved successful.

From the village of Hasparin we were removed about a mile, to the deserted palace of some Gascon nobleman, where we were quartered until the 6th of January, when we advanced, and drove in the enemy's outposts; but returning on the 7th, we did not again move until the middle of February.

While in Hasparin the weather was bad, and we were much harassed, marching a distance of two or three miles every morning to the alarm-post two hours before daylight, and remaining there until it appeared. The inhabitants of the province we were now in were different in dress and manners from both Spaniards and French, but their language seemed to our ears harsh and discordant. The round bonnets of the men, and the dress and healthy look of the women, was much similar to the Scottish peasantry.

I am not certain whether it was here or in Ustaritz—the latter, I believe—that we had two men of our division executed; one hanged for robbing an officer's portmanteau, and another shot for presenting his empty piece at a sergeant of the mounted police corps, who acted as assistants to the provost-marshal, and had been attached to the army since the commencement of the last campaign.

Everyone thought he would be pardoned, or at least his sentence commuted, as it was said there was some unnecessary provocation given by the sergeant; but mercy was not extended to him. We were often inclined to think that the provosts-marshal were possessed of more power than they ought to have had, particularly as they were generally men of a description who abused it, and were guided more by caprice and personal pique than any regard to justice. In fact, they seemed to be above all control, doing what they pleased, without being brought to any account, and were often greater robbers than the men they punished.

After leaving this place, we came up with the French on the 23rd of February, near the village of Sauveterre. A river ran between us and the town, over which there was a bridge that they had placed in a state of defence, their army occupying the opposite bank. On the morning of the 24th, our brigade were ordered some way down from the bridge, for the purpose of crossing a ford near a mill. Our light companies, covered by a party of the seventh hussars, first took the river, in a particular part of which there was a strong current, caused by the mill stream. This, together with the large round stones that formed the bottom, caused some difficulty in getting across; but they effected it, and advancing up the bank through a narrow lane, lined a wall on the top of the height. The cavalry then returned, and the right of the brigade had crossed the river, when the enemy, having detached a strong force to oppose our progress, drove in the light troops so precipitately, that in retreating through the lane already mentioned, they were wedged in so closely that they could not move. A number then struck off to the right, and attempted to swim the river, but being carried away with the current, many of them were drowned. Of those who crossed at the ford many were wounded in the river, and losing their footing sunk to rise no more, among whom was a brave young officer of our regiment.

The French had by this time come close down on them, and none would have escaped being killed or taken prisoners had not a brigade of guns been brought down to the edge of the river, and by a heavy fire of grape covered the retreat. On re-crossing, the brigade withdrew under cover of some houses, and on the 25th the division crossed the river on a bridge of boats, the enemy having blown up the stone bridge, and retreated.

In the affair of the 24th, a great number of our men were taken prisoners, exclusive of the killed and wounded. On the 27th, we came up with the enemy again at Orthes, where their whole army had taken up a position, their left resting on the village and heights of Orthes, and right extending to that of St. Boes. The right of our line was composed of the third and sixth divisions, led on by General Picton; the light division, under Baron Alten, formed the centre; and Marshal Beresford, with the fourth and seventh, formed the left. The battle commenced by the latter attacking St. Boes and carrying it; but by reason of the difficult nature of the ground, it was found impracticable to carry the heights. Their whole line was then attacked by the third, fourth, sixth, and light divisions, when the enemy were dislodged from the heights; and Sir Rowland Hill, who, in advancing to join the conflict, saw the French already routed, the more effectually to prevent their escape, pushed forward the second division and cavalry. Their retreat was well conducted at first, but it gradually became disorderly, and in the end a complete flight, many of the conscripts throwing down their arms and deserting.

The French had made a most obstinate resistance at the point which we had to carry, and kept up a severe cannonade on us, by which many of our men were decapitated, in consequence of their firing chain-shot. In one part of the road where they had been driven from the fields, our cavalry had made a furious charge on them, and taken a number of prisoners. The road was almost rendered impassable by the number of arms lying on it.

Near this place lay a sergeant belonging to our light brigade, extended by the side of a French grenadier, their bayonets transfixed in each other, and both dead. Passing Orthes, we followed the retreat of the enemy until we passed through another town, where part of their rear-guard lined the walls of a churchyard, situated a little above the town, and had brought out tables and chairs to stand on while they fired over upon us.

In passing through this village, a shot from one of their cannon shattered the leg of an old midwife while she was crossing the street; the head doctor of our regiment, a skilful and intelligent surgeon, being passing at the time, having inspected the injury, found it necessary to amputate the limb; and although she was far advanced in years, in three weeks after, when we had occasion to pass near the village, she had almost entirely recovered.

Beyond this village, about two miles, we encamped by the roadside, and had not been long encamped, when my friend the corporal of the band, whom I have already mentioned, arrived, bringing with him a child which he had found in a field under peculiar circumstances. As he and a musician of the 83rd regiment were passing along the road, they were attracted by the piteous cries of a French officer, who lay severely wounded in a ditch a short distance from them; he begged for God's sake that they would give him a drink, and as I have already hinted, P——, always ready to follow the dictates of a benevolent heart, gave him some wine from his canteen. It was then dusk, but while he stooped to give the officer the wine, he perceived something moving beneath his cloak, and on drawing it a little aside, he found a fine boy, about four years old, dressed in the English fashion, nestled in beside him. Taking him up in his arms, he asked him his name, when the child replied, "James." The officer entered into an explanation of the matter, and P—— understood enough of the language, to learn that the child came up the road during a heavy fire while our army and the French were engaged. The officer, who had been wounded a little before, seeing the poor child in imminent danger, and in the midst of his own sufferings, feeling interested for his fate, had enticed him off the road, and kept him amused until he fell asleep, when he wrapped him in the corner of his cloak.

The officer expressed the utmost gratitude for P——'s kindness in giving him the wine, but he seemed to feel parting with the boy; nor did the child seem very willing to part with him. With the view, however, of finding out his parents, James was brought home to the camp, and notice being sent to the different divisions of the army, in a few days the child's mother arrived. Her feelings on again finding her child, may be better imagined than described. She stated, that having come into the town in rear of where the armies were engaged, the child had wandered from her knee while she was suckling a younger one, and that she had searched every part of the town for him without being able to get the least trace of the direction he had taken, or what had become of him.

Having children certainly increased the hardships that the poor women were fated to endure; but excess of suffering, which tore asunder every other tie, only rendered maternal love stronger, and it was amazing what hardships were voluntarily endured for the sake of their offspring. I remember one poor fellow of our brigade, whose wife died, and left an infant with him of a few months old, and although he might have got one of the women to take care of it, he preferred taking charge of it himself, and for many a day he trudged along with it sitting on the top of his knapsack. Sickness at length overtook him, and he went to the rear to hospital, carrying the child with him, but what was their fate afterwards I have never been able to learn.

Next morning we left our encampment, and returning by the way we had come, we passed a man of the division on the roadside, who had been hung up to the branch of a tree a few minutes before. According to the current report in the division, he had entered a mill, and asked the miller to sell him some flour, but the miller refusing to sell it, he took it by force; and being caught in the act by someone, who reported the affair to Lord Wellington, he was tried by a general court-martial, and sentenced to death.

For a long time after his trial, he was marched a prisoner with the provost-guard, and he entertained hopes of pardon; but on that morning, without any previous warning, while he was sitting at the fire with some of his fellow prisoners, the provost came in and ordered him to rise, when placing the rope round his neck, he marched him forward on the road a short distance, and hung him up on the branch of a tree.

Examples, perhaps, were necessary, but we were inclined to think that the time was often unfortunately chosen; it was rather an awkward spectacle to greet the eyes of an army the morning after a hard-fought and successful battle; and the poor wretch's fate excited more commiseration that morning, than detestation of his crime.

Some of the men happened to make remarks on the subject— "Pshaw!" said Dennis, who was listening to them, "I don't believe my countryman would do anything of the sort. Sure it's only a dead man he has ordered to be hung up to frighten yees."

"He is dead enough now," said another.

"Do you remember," said a third, "the tickler of a circular that was served out to us after the dreadful retreat from Salamanca—was that your countryman's doings?"

"Troth, I don't know," said Dennis; "but it didn't go well down with us; and if this is the sort of payment we get for beating the French, the best way is to go down on our knees, and promise never to be guilty of the like again."

Chapter 21

Into France

In consequence of the wet weather, we were unable to proceed, and lay in camp near this place for about three weeks; and little of any moment occurred during that time, except the capture of Aire on the 2nd of March, by General Hill's division.

On the 18th March, the enemy having retired in the night upon Vic Bigorre, we advanced on the 19th, and came up with their rear-guard, which was posted in great force in the vineyards in front of that town. Our division, under General Picton, advanced up the main road to the attack, until the enemy's artillery, which commanded it, forced us to strike into the fields to the right and left, when we drove them from one field to another, while they contested every inch of the ground with the greatest obstinacy, at every hedge and ditch giving us a volley as we came up, and then retreating to the next fence.

While advancing upon one of these temporary defences, a French soldier, through some cause, was rather tardy in retreating, and our men were close upon him before he started out of the ditch. His comrades had, by this time, lined the fence farther on, and being a remarkable object, a number of our skirmishers directed their fire against him; but he did not seem much incommoded, for after running a few paces, he turned about and fired on his pursuers; and reloading his piece, continued this running fire for some distance. His daring conduct having attracted the attention of all, a great number joined in trying to bring the poor fellow down, and the shot was flying about him in every direction; but he seemed invulnerable. At length, coming near to where his own party was under cover, he walked up to the edge of the embankment, and after firing at the party who were in his rear, he clapped his hand very contemptuously on his breech, and jumped down into the ditch.

Those to the left of the road, being brought to a point by a river, were obliged to cross the main road, where they suffered severely. A sergeant of our brigade received a dreadful wound here—a cannon-shot having struck him, carried away the fleshy part of the thigh, leaving the bone perfectly bare, to the extent of twelve or fourteen inches. A little farther on, a lad belonging to the band of the 83rd regiment lay killed. The band in general accompanied the baggage, but he never would submit to this; and when near the enemy, he always did duty with the light company.

Having driven the enemy from the vineyards, in retreating through the town they killed a number of our men, from the various places they had got under cover. One poor fellow of the 5th regiment received a shot, which, passing through his temples, cut the strings of his eyes, and we saw him sitting on a stone with them hanging out of their sockets. The whole of our army having assembled that night at Vic Bigorre and Rabastains, the enemy retired in the night upon Tarbes, and we came up with their advanced posts in that town on the 20th; their centre and left had retired, and their right was attacked by the sixth division under General Clinton, while General Hill attacked the hill by the high road from Vic Bigorre.

The sixth division being successful, General Hill passed through the town, and disposed his columns for attack, when the enemy retreated in all directions, having suffered severely, while our loss was but trifling. Following them up the Garonne as far as Grenada, on the 8th of April a pontoon bridge was thrown across, and the eighteenth hussars, with a Portuguese and Spanish brigade, crossed, and drove in a body of the enemy's cavalry, taking about a hundred prisoners.

The town of Toulouse is surrounded on three sides by the canal of Languedoc and the Garonne. They had fortified the suburbs on the left of that river with strong field-works; they had likewise formed works at each bridge of the canal, defended by artillery and musketry. Beyond the canal, to the eastward, and between that and the river Ers, there is a range of heights extending for some distance, over which pass all the roads to the canal and town from the eastward, which it defends; and the enemy, in addition to the outworks at the bridges of the canal, had fortified the heights with five redoubts connected by lines of entrenchments; they had also broken all the bridges over the river Ers within our reach, by which the right of their position could be approached. When the Spanish corps passed, the pontoon bridge was moved higher up, in order to shorten the communication with General Hill's division, and this was done so late on the evening of the 9th, that the attack was delayed till next day.

Our division crossed on the evening of the 9th, and next morning, the troops under Marshal Beresford attacked the enemy's right, while the Spaniards under General Frere assailed the centre; but the latter were soon repulsed, and being, with a heavy loss, driven from the ground, were pursued to some distance. By the exertions of their officers, however, they were formed anew, when our light division, which was immediately on their right, took up their place. In the mean time, Beresford, with the fourth and sixth divisions, attacked and carried the heights on the enemy's right, and the redoubt which covered and protected that flank, and lodged his troops in the redoubt. The enemy, however, still occupied the others.

As soon as the Spaniards had re-formed, and were brought back to the attack, General Beresford continued his march along the ridge, and carried, with General Pack's brigade, the two principal redoubts, and the fortified houses in the enemy's centre. The enemy made a desperate effort from the canal to regain those redoubts, but were repulsed with considerable loss; and the sixth division continuing their movement along the ridge, and the Spanish troops on the front, the enemy were driven from all their redoubts and entrenchments on the left, and the whole range of heights were in our possession.

While these operations were going on on the left, General Hill drove the enemy from their exterior works in the suburb on the left of the Garonne, within the old wall. Our division charged the works at the bridges, but, in consequence of their strength, were unable to carry them, and suffered severely in the attempt.

During the 11th, not a shot was fired on either side, and the French bands were playing the greater part of the day. Ours were also brought down, and a sort of conversation was kept up by the different tunes played. The French would listen attentively while ours played *The Downfall of Paris*, and in turn gave us a reply of the same kind. Next morning, to our surprise, we found them gone. They had retreated during the night, leaving in our hands three generals and one thousand six hundred prisoners, with much stores of all descriptions.

On the evening of the 12th an express arrived from Paris, to inform Lord Wellington of the peace; Marshal Soult would not believe it, but he agreed to a cessation of hostilities. We were now encamped at the outside of the town, where we remained for a few days. When advancing about three leagues, we met a messenger on his way to Toulouse, on a mission from the government, and it was now that we got full confirmation of the joyful news. Each heart beat light at the intelligence, hut we could scarcely dare to believe it; we had been so often deceived, that we thought it too good news to be true. Nothing, however, was now talked of but home.

We were quartered in Le Mas, a short distance from Toulouse, where we remained until the order came for us to march to Blanchefort, situated in one of the sandy plains of the Landes. The land was incapable of cultivation, but they fed numerous flocks of sheep on it, and the shepherds were mounted on huge stilts to enable them to see for some distance around. The whole army being collected here, the different individuals who had formerly been acquainted, had an opportunity of seeing each other, and our meeting was the happier that we could now congratulate each other on the return of peace.

In marching from Toulouse to this place, we parted with the

Portuguese army at Condom. They were then well regulated and well disciplined troops. The English mode of discipline had been introduced among them for some time, a number of English officers were attached to them; and acting always in concert with us, they were now little inferior to ourselves. A kind of friendship had thus arisen, and caused us to feel sorry at parting. On the morning that this happened, they were ranged upon the street, and saluted us as we passed, and their hearty *"Vivas!"* and exclamations of regret, evinced that they really felt: but a scene of a more affecting nature took place in the Portuguese and Spanish women parting with the men of our army, to whom they had attached themselves during the miserable state of their country. The generality of them were not married, but the steady affection and patient endurance of hardship which they exhibited, in following those to whom they belonged, would have done credit to a more legal tie. Being here ordered to return to their own country with the Portuguese army, and strict orders given to prevent any of them from proceeding farther, the scene which ensued was distressing—the poor creatures running about concealing themselves, in the vain hope of being allowed to remain; but it was all to no purpose: although they were willing to have sacrificed country and relations to follow us, the sacrifice could not be accepted.

From Blanchefort camp we proceeded to Pauilhac, from whence, in a few days, we embarked in small vessels, which took us down to the Corduan lighthouse, where we were put on board the *San Domingo*, 74 gun ship, and after a pleasant passage arrived at the Cove of Cork, where we disembarked.

Our regiment was nearly nine hundred strong when we first went out to the Peninsula. During the time we remained there, we received at various times recruits to the amount of four hundred, and when we left the country, our strength was about two hundred and fifty, out of which number not more than one hundred and fifty remained who went out with the regiment.

CHAPTER 22

Conclusion

I have thus endeavoured, as far as my recollection served me, to give a simple and faithful description of those scenes in which I was myself an actor, without partiality to any class. If occasionally I have drawn an unseemly picture, the fault was in the original, for I have no personal enmity to any individual in the service; and I beg it may be distinctly understood, that many of the abuses which I have narrated are only spoken of as things that have existed, rather than as a picture of the present state of the army. Thanks to his Royal Highness the commander-in-chief, little is now left the soldier to complain of.

When we look back twenty or thirty years, and consider what the army was then, and what it is now, the wonder will be, not that it is not in a better state, but that so much has been done to ameliorate the condition of the soldier. Then he was one of the veriest slaves existing, obliged to rise two or three hours before day to commence his cleaning operations. His hair required to be soaped, floured, and frizzed, or tortured into some uncouth shape which gave him acute pain, and robbed him of all power of moving his head, unless he brought his body round with it. He had his musket to burnish, his cap and cartridge-box to polish with heel-ball, and his white breeches to pipe-clay, so that it generally required three or four hours hard labour to prepare him for parade; and when he turned out, he was like something made of glass, which the slightest accident might derange or break to pieces.

He was then subjected to a rigid inspection, in which, if a single hair stood out of its place, extra guard, drill, or some other punishment awaited him. When to this was added the supercilious tyrannical demeanour of his superiors, who seemed to look upon him as a brute animal who had neither soul nor feeling, and who caned or flogged him without mercy for the slightest offence, we cannot wonder that he became the debased being, in body and mind, which they already considered him, or that he possessed the common vices of a slave—fawning servility, duplicity, and want of all self-respect; to add to this, what was his reward when worn out and unfit for further service?—a pittance insufficient to support nature, or a pass to beg.

When we consider that, in the face of long established usages, and coadjutors of unbending and contracted views of human nature, the commander-in-chief by his persevering exertions has almost entirely abolished those numerous vexations—when we see gentlemanly feeling and attention to the soldier's best interests encouraged among the officers of the army, and the change wrought in the moral and military character of the soldier by these means—is it to be wondered at that every individual in the service is attached to the Duke of York, and looks up to him in the light of a father and a friend. Few generals of whom I have ever either heard or read, enjoyed the esteem and affection of the troops under their command more than His Royal Highness.

LEONAUR

ALSO FROM LEONAUR
AVAILABLE IN SOFTCOVER OR HARDCOVER WITH DUST JACKET

CAPTAIN OF THE 95th (Rifles) by Jonathan Leach—An officer of Wellington's Sharpshooters during the Peninsular, South of France and Waterloo Campaigns of the Napoleonic Wars.

BUGLER AND OFFICER OF THE RIFLES by William Green & Harry Smith With the 95th (Rifles) during the Peninsular & Waterloo Campaigns of the Napoleonic Wars

BAYONETS, BUGLES AND BONNETS by James 'Thomas' Todd—Experiences of hard soldiering with the 71st Foot - the Highland Light Infantry - through many battles of the Napoleonic wars including the Peninsular & Waterloo Campaigns

THE ADVENTURES OF A LIGHT DRAGOON by George Farmer & G.R. Gleig—A cavalryman during the Peninsular & Waterloo Campaigns, in captivity & at the siege of Bhurtpore, India

THE COMPLEAT RIFLEMAN HARRIS by Benjamin Harris as told to & transcribed by Captain Henry Curling—The adventures of a soldier of the 95th (Rifles) during the Peninsular Campaign of the Napoleonic Wars

WITH WELLINGTON'S LIGHT CAVALRY by William Tomkinson—The Experiences of an officer of the 16th Light Dragoons in the Peninsular and Waterloo campaigns of the Napoleonic Wars.

SURTEES OF THE RIFLES by William Surtees—A Soldier of the 95th (Rifles) in the Peninsular campaign of the Napoleonic Wars.

ENSIGN BELL IN THE PENINSULAR WAR by George Bell—The Experiences of a young British Soldier of the 34th Regiment 'The Cumberland Gentlemen' in the Napoleonic wars.

WITH THE LIGHT DIVISION by John H. Cooke—The Experiences of an Officer of the 43rd Light Infantry in the Peninsula and South of France During the Napoleonic Wars

NAPOLEON'S IMPERIAL GUARD: FROM MARENGO TO WATERLOO by J. T. Headley—This is the story of Napoleon's Imperial Guard from the bearskin caps of the grenadiers to the flamboyance of their mounted chasseurs, their principal characters and the men who commanded them.

BATTLES & SIEGES OF THE PENINSULAR WAR by W. H. Fitchett—Corunna, Busaco, Albuera, Ciudad Rodrigo, Badajos, Salamanca, San Sebastian & Others

www.ingramcontent.com/pod-product-compliance
Lightning Source LLC
Chambersburg PA
CBHW032051080426
42733CB00006B/236